Contents

Acknowledgements

I would like to thank:

Leeds Early Years Development and Childcare Partnership for the opportunity to work as a Partnership Advisory Teacher within the city. It is a privilege to be part of such a motivated and dedicated team and I continue to learn from my colleagues and the settings I visit.

The children and staff at Cottingley Primary School, Leeds, who are always keen to try new ideas and will recognise many of the activities in this book. Also to the parents who have given permission for photographs of their children to be used.

The staff, children and parents at Fortis Green Nursery in London for giving permission to use photographs.

Community Playthings for supplying photographs of their excellent play equipment.

The team at David Fulton Publishers and, in particular, Nina Stibbe for her support.

My family for their patience and continued interest in my work.

QCA for permission to use extracts from 'Curriculum Guidance for the Foundation Stage'.

Organising Play in the Early Years

Practical Ideas and Activities for all Practitioners

JANE DRAKE

David Fulton Publishers

David Fulton Publishers Ltd
The Chiswick Centre, 414 Chiswick High Road, London W4 5TF

www.fultonpublishers.co.uk

David Fulton Publishers is a division of Granada Learning Limited,
part of ITV plc.

British Library Cataloguing in Publication Data
A catalogue record for this book is available from the British Library.

ISBN 1 84312 025 9

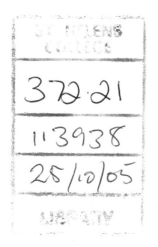
Typeset by Keyset Composition, Colchester, Essex
Printed and bound in Great Britain by Ashford Colour Press Limited,
Gosport, Hants.

To my husband, Fred

Introduction

The quality of the learning environment is a crucial factor in what and how children learn. As early years practitioners, we should be aiming to provide an environment that is exciting and motivating, and that challenges all children in the setting appropriately, enabling them to make progress from their own starting point. It should encourage children to initiate their own learning and to develop ideas and interests over time.

The environment offered by many early years settings is organised into areas (such as sand, water and construction), which will be referred to in this book as 'areas of provision'. Of course, in any well-planned area of provision there will be opportunities for learning across the foundation stage curriculum, and certainly the early learning goals for personal, social and emotional development should underpin all learning. But when planning provision in a setting, it is a good idea to identify key areas of learning promoted through each area of provision. This is a decision for teams within each setting. It may be that one setting decides to focus on mathematical development, physical development and creative development when planning provision in the sand area, whereas another may identify knowledge and understanding of the world and mathematical development as key areas. The important thing is that there is a breadth and balance of learning across the whole provision. The long-term planning for provision should involve the whole team and be viewed as a developmental process – it is the thought and decision-making that goes into the planning that makes it so valuable. Reviewing the plans regularly is also an important part of the process of 'moving forward'.

Where practical constraints dictate that it is not possible to provide all areas every day, teams need to think carefully about how they organise certain provision on a rotational basis. Children's learning will be of a higher quality if they are able to return to experiences and activities over time, revisiting and extending ideas and consolidating their understanding. It is much more effective to offer an area for a whole week and then to offer another for a similar length of time than to offer both on alternate days throughout the whole two-week period.

When practitioners are secure in the knowledge that, through the basic, continuous provision they are offering, children are able to make progress towards the early learning goals in all areas of the curriculum, they will recognise the importance of spending time with children in those areas of provision. The adults' role when working in an area will vary according to need. They will sometimes be observing in order to assess children's learning and support their next steps, and at other times involving themselves in children's spontaneous play. There are many ways of supporting child-initiated learning – it may be by providing extra resources to enhance or extend their play or by challenging their thinking through carefully framed questions. Sometimes it is right to keep your distance and, if all the children disappear from the area as you enter, you can be fairly sure that you have adopted the wrong approach! It is not always easy to assess the situation, but it is by observing and listening to children that the necessary skills are developed.

The focus activities included in each chapter are examples of how practitioners can motivate or support children's learning through an adult-led or initiated activity in a particular area of provision. In any early years setting, practitioners will probably plan such focus activities to tie in with predictable interests, topics or themes, and certainly in response to children's observed interests and needs. They may also draw on ideas included in long-term plans for areas of provision. These examples of activities can be adapted for use in a range of settings, but it is important to emphasise that children will always bring their own experiences and learning interests to an activity. Practitioners must be prepared to respond spontaneously in order effectively to support individuals' developing knowledge and understanding.

The omission of a separate chapter on ICT in this book does not mean that this area of learning has been in any way ignored or marginalized. Providing for children's development in ICT is not merely about including a computer in the setting but about finding appropriate ways of enabling them to explore a range of equipment and everyday purposes in the context of their play. Opportunities for learning about ICT in areas of provision are included in other chapters.

If provision is thoughtfully planned, opportunities for developing mathematical ideas and methods in a context will be plentiful throughout the setting as a whole, and particularly rich in certain areas. Children's self-initiated play will provide them with numerous mathematical, problem-solving challenges; for example, in the technology workshop 'How long does my piece of tape need to be to go around the box?' and in the construction area 'How many bricks high does the bridge need to be to allow the car to pass under it?' Some practitioners offer a maths/number area in addition to these opportunities, and it can be useful for children to have access to a central base for resources and an area where they are able to explore equipment and also from which they can select to develop ideas and solve problems in other areas. Such an area would probably include equipment such as number lines, grids, dice, number 'spinners', solid and flat shapes, number inset trays, number rhymes and books, beads and buttons, sorting equipment, interesting items to count (e.g. polished stones, shells), pegs and pegboards and an abacus.

Practitioners should look carefully at how equipment is organised across the setting and the learning they can promote through self-selection and tidying-up routines, particularly in the areas of personal, social and emotional development, communication, language and literacy and mathematical development. Deciding on criteria for sorting into storage boxes, selecting from, and replacing equipment on, shaped and numbered templates and accessing information from labels on trays and boxes are all activities rich in learning opportunities. In taking responsibility for the daily care and organisation of equipment, children are also developing independence skills.

Sometimes a 'tabletop' area may be provided for activities such as jigsaws and games. However, it is important to guard against an over-emphasis on jigsaws. Although they can offer valuable learning potential, other activities, such as replacing equipment on templated surfaces, can often achieve the same learning outcomes and become part of the daily routine.

Whether offering sessional or full day-care, settings will make provision for children to participate in 'snack time', involving a drink and perhaps something to eat. This activity can provide opportunities for developing healthy eating habits and social skills but can also offer a valuable forum for discussion and sharing of experiences. A permanent 'snack' area is often set up within the setting, with children encouraged to access this independently, perhaps pouring their own juice or selecting their milk carton. Cups and cartons can be identified with individual tags or labels and a system of clearing away afterwards introduced. Periods will be planned for adults to spend time with children in the area preparing and sharing food and talking with children. The advantage of continuous provision in this area is that children will be able to access it at a time that is appropriate for them, when they are ready and receptive. They will not need to be withdrawn from an activity, with which they may be deeply involved, in order to take part in a whole-group 'timetabled' snack time.

The sharing of ideas is vital in the development of good practice. Very few of our initiatives or practical innovations are truly original. Although it is not always a conscious process, most are adapted or evolve from what we have observed in other settings or absorbed on courses, or are inspired through discussion with colleagues. Of course, there is always the possibility that two practitioners in two different settings working towards the same aim will come up with the same practical way of achieving that aim. It is not uncommon for practitioners to think they have come up with a brilliant new idea only to discover something very similar at the setting down the road. It is important to recognise that there is always something to learn when planning the environment for children, and setting up systems for sharing information and practice should be a priority for teams. The content of this book is offered, and intended, not as a prescriptive framework but as a model, and a vehicle for sharing practical ideas for good early years practice. Settings are individual, each with its own strengths, needs and constraints. This book aims to be adaptable to the full range of settings.

1 Construction and small world

Introduction to the area

Children need plenty of space in the construction area if they are to develop their ideas and work collaboratively. A cramped area is limiting and inevitably leads to frustration. There must be enough room to allow children to move freely around their constructions and to access equipment as their work progresses. A large area also allows for the possibility of two or three individual projects taking place at the same time. Ideally, the area should be carpeted, as children may spend considerable lengths of time sitting or kneeling as they work.

In order to provide the very large space necessary for certain construction projects – for example, building a castle using cardboard boxes from the supermarket – practitioners may plan for these particular activities to take place in the outdoor area, and suggestions for appropriate equipment can be found in Chapter 11.

Indoor provision should include construction equipment that helps to develop a range of skills and concepts. There are numerous kits on the market and, before making a financial commitment, practitioners should consider carefully what learning will be promoted through each kit, how kits will complement each other and, very importantly, how durable components will be. It is much better to build up stock in a few, carefully chosen, kits over time than to provide a limited selection of components in a large range of kits. A set of maple wood blocks is always a valuable addition to provision and, although a big investment, will offer high quality learning experiences and will last for years. It is also a good idea to supplement construction equipment with recycled materials such as cardboard boxes and packaging.

The nature of children's work in the construction area often means that they will want to return to projects over a period of time to review and modify their work. It is a good idea to designate an area where children can display work in progress, and know that it will not be handled by others without their permission.

Many practitioners include some small world equipment in the construction area, and children should certainly have access to such equipment as they work in this area. Others choose to provide a separate area for small world equipment and, if space allows, this can enable practitioners to offer children a wider range of opportunities and serve as a central resource base for other areas, e.g. sea world creatures in the water area. If the construction and small world areas are linked, or positioned adjacent to each other, opportunities for developing imaginative ideas in both will be enriched – cars made from kit components come to life if they are able to carry passengers (small world people), and stories of fantastic journeys can

A cardboard box castle in the construction area

soon evolve! The two sets of equipment will also enable children to construct with a design purpose in mind: for example, 'Can we build a garage (from blocks in the construction area) big enough to accommodate this car (from small world equipment)?'

Small world equipment can be stored in 'themed' boxes. If space is limited or practitioners decide to focus on a particular environment, some of these boxes can be offered on a rotational basis, although equipment such as vehicles and people should probably be available permanently.

Basic resources

Furniture and storage

- Storage units. Wheeled trolleys containing sliding plastic trays or boxes are ideal, as they offer a surface to work, or to display models/small world environments on, as well as storage. Label trays or boxes clearly. Photographs cut out from catalogues alongside words make information accessible to young children.
- Wall shelves or open shelving units for displays of children's work, books, objects of interest or templated equipment (e.g. wooden blocks).
- A round table may be appropriate in the small world area so that children can build collaboratively or work cooperatively around an environment displayed in a large, round, shallow tray.

Equipment and materials

Construction

- Wooden blocks, solid and hollow.
- Small-scale wooden planks.
- Construction kits (including, for example, cogs and wheels, interlocking bricks, nuts and bolts, connectors).
- Tape measures and rulers.
- Play tools (e.g. drill, screwdriver, pliers, spanner), hard hats.
- Clipboards, paper, mark-making tools.
- Folded card (to make name cards to identify models).
- Ring file and plastic pockets for children's plans and drawings.

Small world

- Mark-making equipment, scissors, pieces of card (to make signs or labels).
- Small and large shallow trays, open cardboard boxes (e.g. shoeboxes), plastic tanks – to be used as bases for creating environments.
- People (reflecting a range of ages and ethnicity).
- Cars, lorries, vans, tractors, diggers, caravans, bikes.
- Boats, aeroplanes.
- Train and track.
- Sea creatures, jungle animals, farm animals, insects, dinosaurs.
- Trees, plastic pondweed, imitation plants.

- Box containing pieces of fabric.
- Plastic jars or boxes containing materials such as pea gravel, cotton wool, pebbles, bubble wrap.
- Lengths of imitation grass.

What will the children do and learn?

Construction

- Explore and compare solid and flat shapes through block play, and begin to use the language of shape.
- Look closely at the attributes of bricks or components and sort according to shape, colour or size.
- Use language such as 'long', 'short', 'heavy', 'big' or 'bigger' to describe and compare length, weight and size.
- Count reliably (e.g. 'How many blocks did you use to build your tower?'), begin to estimate ('How many blocks do you think you will need to build a tower as tall as the castle?') and use language such as 'one more'.
- Build with a design or purpose in mind.
- Understand the functions/purposes of certain parts and components and select appropriately for a task.
- Give and receive verbal instructions.
- Follow picture instructions and simple diagrams.
- Explain to others the purpose of, or how they have made, their model.
- Record ideas or plans on paper.
- Dismantle models.
- Develop physical skills through the handling and use of small equipment.
- Work creatively to build imaginative constructions or develop story ideas through construction and small world equipment.
- Work collaboratively with others on a project.
- Return to models over a period of time to review and make modifications.

Small world

- Recreate environments, or 'worlds', building on first-hand experience.
- Revisit experiences.
- Represent imaginative ideas.
- Develop ideas over a period of time.
- Retell familiar stories, talking about key characters and events.
- Make up their own stories.
- Use language to express ideas and thoughts.

- Increase knowledge about other parts of the world, climates and cultures.
- Talk about features of small world creatures they handle.
- Develop fine motor skills through manipulation of small objects.

Display tips

Construction area

- Architects' plans, e.g. for new houses, displayed alongside photographs or artists' impressions of completed houses.
- Photographs of construction sites and buildings in progress.
- Photographs of buildings, including different designs and purposes.
- Photographs of nursery equipment being assembled (e.g. a new bike or piece of furniture), alongside diagrams and instructions.
- Photographs of children's constructions and plans with, where appropriate, lists of components and equipment used.
- Shelf display of children's models.
- Interactive display of mechanical toys or toys with moving parts.
- Catalogue photographs of power tools.
- Street and road maps of the local area.

Small world

- Photographs of real environments, e.g. rainforest, desert, city, arctic.
- Photographs of children's own made environments in progress and comments scribed during their play.
- Favourite stories with photographs of small world play related to these, e.g. 'We're going on a bear hunt', 'Red Riding Hood'.
- Photographic examples of how small world equipment has been used in other areas of provision.
- Children's drawings of their small world environments and imaginative ideas, perhaps sequenced in a 'storyline'.
- Photographic examples of representation, e.g. 'Tom used a pineapple top as a tree in his tropical world'.

Possible links with other areas of provision

Construction

Technology workshop

Children may find materials from the workshop useful in their building work. Encourage them to select boxes, tubes etc. according to the needs of their 'project'.

Office

To encourage links between these two areas, set up a builders' office providing equipment such as order forms for building materials, plan formats, builders' merchants' catalogues, construction workers' telephone numbers, invoice pads. Take telephone messages that offer children challenges, e.g. 'That was Mrs Jackson – she needs a new kennel for her dog. It must be big enough for him to sleep in and must keep him dry. Can you build one?' In this case, provide a soft toy dog so that children can design the kennel to specifications.

Small world

Book area

Use small world equipment to support children's exploration of stories and alongside non-fiction books, e.g. about farms or forests.

Sand

Provide small world equipment, such as dinosaurs, imitation or real potted plants, twigs and small branches, stones, gravel and pebbles, to create a 'Jurassic' environment.

Focus activities in the construction and small world areas

Building bridges (construction)

Remote-control toys are always popular and there should be no shortage of volunteers for this activity. Challenge children to build a bridge high and wide enough for their car and then ask them to steer it underneath.

Building bridges (construction)

Key areas of learning	Mathematical development (shape, space and measures). Knowledge and understanding of the world (designing and making skills, information and communication technology).
Key early learning goals	Use developing mathematical ideas and methods to solve practical problems. Build and construct with a wide range of objects, selecting appropriate resources and adapting their work where necessary. Find out about and identify the uses of everyday technology and use information and communication technology and programmable toys to support their learning.
Resources needed/ enhancements to provision	A range of construction equipment, including commercially produced kits and materials such as cardboard boxes and tubes. Remote-control car. Roll of paper.
Preparation	Make sure that children have plenty of space to work – constructions may be large, and control of the car initially unpredictable. Introduce children to the necessary directional vocabulary beforehand and ensure that they are familiar with the meaning of any control symbols on the handset (e.g. arrows). It is a good idea to give children experience of using symbols in another context before introducing the equipment; for example, following a trail of arrow signs in the outdoor area. Allow children time to experiment with the remote-control car before challenging them to build the bridge.
Key vocabulary	Directional vocabulary: forwards, backwards, stop, start, left, right. Positional vocabulary: in front, behind, next to, in, on, under. Measurement vocabulary: big, small, long, short, wide, narrow, tall, short. Shape vocabulary: circle, square, triangle, rectangle, cylinder, cone, cube, cuboid.
Activity content	Handling and talking about construction equipment and materials. Discussing plans. Selecting appropriate equipment for the task. Comparing the height or width of the car with the length of blocks etc. Building bridge constructions. Testing constructions using a remote-control car. Modifying constructions. Building a number of bridges across a paper roadway and following the route with the car. Practising and developing control skills when operating the car.
Adult role	Demonstrate the skills needed to control the car. Support children as they become familiar with controls. Model use of key vocabulary. Challenge children's thinking through comments and questions, e.g. 'How could you make the bridge a little bit taller?' 'Why do you think it falls down so easily? How could we make it stronger?'
Follow-up ideas	Mark chalk roadways on the ground in the outdoor area. Support children in building a 'town' around the road, making bridges, traffic lights, zebra crossings and buildings. Encourage them to 'drive' the remote-control car through the 'town', turning, stopping and starting as appropriate.

Billy Goats Gruff (small world)

This traditional story is a favourite with most young children and can provide an appealing starting point for small world play. Use turf for the field and add an exciting realism to the environment!

Small world Billy Goats Gruff

Billy Goats Gruff (small world)

Key areas of learning	Communication, language and literacy (reading).
	Creative development (imagination).
Key early learning goals	Retell narratives in the correct sequence, drawing on language patterns of stories.
	Show an understanding of the elements of stories, such as main character, sequence of events and openings, and how information can be found in non-fiction texts to answer questions about where, who, why and how.
	Use their imagination in art and design, music, dance, imaginative play, role-play and stories.
Resources needed/ enhancements to provision	A copy of the traditional story 'The Three Billy Goats Gruff'.
	A large, shallow tray (a builder's mixing tray is ideal and can be purchased at reasonable cost from DIY stores or builders' merchants).
	Pieces of turf.
	Pebbles, stones and gravel.
	Potted plants.
	Three small plastic goats (graded in size).
	A troll.
	A bridge (this could be made in the technology workshop by children).
	Coconut shells (or other items that can be used to produce a 'trip, trap' sound).
Preparation	Share the story of 'The Three Billy Goats Gruff' with children.
	Prepare the small world environment using turf to represent the field, gravel as paths and potted plants as trees.

Key vocabulary	Big, middle-sized, small.
	Goat, troll, bridge.
	Encourage children to use repeated phrases, such as 'Who's that trip-trapping over my bridge?'
Activity content	Showing interest in, and handling, small world equipment.
	Engaging in imaginative play.
	Retelling the story of 'The Three Billy Goats Gruff' using the small world props.
	Taking on character roles.
	Talking about key events in the story.
	Modifying the environment as play develops.
	Making up their own stories, or variations of the familiar story, using the props.
Adult role	Support children in retelling the story of 'The Three Billy Goats Gruff', referring to the book illustrations when appropriate.
	Play alongside children, modelling imaginative ideas and story making.
	Encourage children to develop their own story ideas, asking open-ended questions.
	Take photographs of children's play at different stages.
Follow-up ideas	Water the turf daily and it will continue to grow for a while, adding another interest to the activity.
	Use photographs of the children's play as illustrations when compiling a 'Billy Goats Gruff' book. This book could then be kept in the book area.
	Add other small world characters to the environment to encourage children to develop their own story ideas.

2 Technology workshop

Introduction to the area

The technology workshop is an area where children can explore materials and develop the thinking and practical skills involved in designing and making. Children often work very creatively in this area but to do so they need access to a wide variety of tools and materials. When organising the area, practitioners should allow enough space for storage of the full range of equipment and carefully consider safety issues. Positioning the workshop in an open 'thoroughfare' where children are continually walking past is more likely to lead to accidents with tools than is a more 'protected' space. Other factors that can impact on the safety of the area are children's knowledge of how to handle and use tools, and whether or not they are able to concentrate sufficiently as they work. In order to minimise the risks, and also to ensure effective use of equipment, practitioners must spend time teaching skills and safety rules, and modelling appropriate use of tools. They should, as far as possible, provide an area that is free from distractions.

The key to organising materials effectively is to set up an efficient storage system and to be clear about staff responsibilities regarding the replenishing of stock. Children are very enthusiastic consumers and the technology workshop can be a high maintenance area! Parents and carers are usually generous suppliers and 'reminder' notes when stocks are low generally result in a large delivery. Check materials as they arrive – make sure that food containers are washed well and be vigilant in disposing of items such as bottles or packets that have contained tablets or medicines. It is a good idea to make clear to parents the kind of resources you are looking for in a letter home, or a poster in the setting. This could include a 'prompt' about safety issues.

Sorting materials into, for example, plastics, card, cork, paper and fabric will be a valuable learning experience for children and it is a good idea to involve them in 'stocking up' the area. In order for children to be able to sort, and for them to make appropriate selections, containers should be clearly labelled (with pictures or examples of materials and words) and should be easily accessible. Tools that are part of the permanent provision can be presented on vertical (hanging up) or horizontal templated surfaces. Other tools, such as hammers and hacksaws, may be kept in a storage cupboard and only provided under adult supervision.

As in the construction area, children will want to develop ideas and add to models over time, and it is important to offer a display area for their work. The provision of mark-making tools and sticky labels or folded card will encourage children to identify their own work.

The outdoor area will probably offer children opportunities to work on a much larger scale, perhaps with cardboard boxes from the supermarket. The natural materials found outside can also be used in, for example, weaving projects – twigs, leaves and grasses woven by children into a willow frame can provide them with very valuable learning experiences, particularly in the areas of creative development and knowledge and understanding of the world. Practitioners should be aware of such possibilities when planning provision.

Basic resources

Furniture and storage

- Practical containers for storing materials such as corks, ribbon, plastic bottle lids e.g. shallow plastic baskets, plastic 'sweet jars', sea-grass baskets, plastic stacking boxes or small wooden drawer units. (Sweet jars can be used very effectively as wool or string dispensers. A ball of string is placed in the jar and the end is threaded through a hole (drilled by an adult) in the lid. The lid is tightened and children pull string through the hole, cutting off the required length. (This system can help to avoid frustrating tangling.)
- Open-shelved unit or trolley.
- Larger container for cardboard boxes. Where space is at a premium, perhaps a plastic, wheeled container could be kept under the table and pulled out when in use. Alternatively, cardboard boxes could be opened out and flattened.
- Storage containers for materials such as cardboard tubes or paper art straws. Waste-paper bins or plastic spaghetti jars can be useful.

- Suitable storage containers for scissors and glue spreaders. Alternatively, tools such as these could be kept on templated shelves.
- Trays or baskets for paper and card.
- Table – large enough for children to work on large, collaborative projects together. A protective table cover if required.
- An area (perhaps an extra table or a wall shelf) designated for children's work in progress.

Equipment and materials

- Washable aprons.
- Paper and card of various thicknesses and finishes. Textured wallpaper can provide interesting surfaces.
- Cellophane, foil, plastic.
- Paper art straws, rolled-up newspaper, paper towel cardboard tubes.
- Offcuts of wood, pieces of dowel, wooden 'lolly' sticks.
- A range of fabrics, e.g. hessian, velvet, cotton, satin.
- Threads, e.g. ribbon, cord, wool, string, embroidery threads.
- Plastic webbing (to be used for sewing or weaving). Large-scale garden webbing set in a free standing wooden frame makes a very effective weaving frame.
- Plastic containers, e.g. yoghurt pots, drinks bottles.
- Cardboard containers, e.g. cereal boxes.
- Plastic lids.
- Corks.
- Natural materials such as shells and twigs.
- Glue. Different types of glue will serve different purposes and offer varying experiences, e.g. glue sticks, PVA glue, non-fungicidal paste.
- Tape, e.g. masking tape, sticky tape.
- Treasury tags, paper clips, wooden pegs, pipe-cleaners, split pins.
- Scissors. These should be suitable for use by children but should cut effectively. Double-handled scissors or sprung 'snips' can be easier to use.
- Glue spreaders.
- Hole punches.
- Clipboards.
- Mark-making tools.
- Sticky labels and folded card (to enable children to identify their own work).

What will children do and learn?

- Explore materials using appropriate senses.
- Look closely at, and compare, texture, shape and pattern in materials.
- Become aware of properties of materials and use this knowledge when making selections.
- Explore the media of collage.
- Learn safe and appropriate use of tools.
- Develop skills of joining, cutting (or tearing) and folding.
- Use correct names for tools and equipment and language such as 'long', 'longer'.
- Dismantle and re-form cardboard boxes, developing an understanding of nets.
- Experiment with ideas and techniques.
- Represent imaginative ideas.
- Make functional models.
- Plan in advance and share design ideas with others.
- Give and receive verbal instructions.
- Making drawings or plans of models on paper.
- Modify work in response to observations.

Display tips

- Shelf display of children's finished models or work in progress.
- Photographs of children's work at various stages in its development, with written explanations and children's scribed comments.
- Cardboard boxes, e.g. cereal boxes displayed alongside their nets (collect two of each box in advance).
- Posters of artists' work in three-dimensions or collage work, e.g. work by Barbara Hepworth, Henri Matisse.
- Interactive displays, including everyday objects made from a variety of materials, e.g. wooden, metal, plastic. Alternatively, a range of objects all produced from the same material could be provided.
- 'Tactile' display – pieces of fabric attached to a surface within children's comfortable reach so that they can feel, and compare, textures.

Possible links with other areas of provision

Paint

Children may want to paint models they make in the technology workshop and, when organising provision, many practitioners position these two areas adjacent to each other. Children can also use items such as bottle tops and corks from the technology workshop when exploring printing techniques.

Office

Some of the equipment provided in the technology workshop can be duplicated in the office area, offering children another context in which to develop the skills of design and technology, e.g. treasury tags, hole punches, glue sticks and sticky tape.

Music and sound

The technology workshop is an ideal area for children to extend their 'sound' investigations by experimenting with different materials in containers and making their own musical instruments.

Focus activities in the technology workshop

Making connections

Encourage children to explore different ways of joining and fixing materials (other than glue and tape) and display their mobiles for others to learn from.

Making connections	
Key areas of learning	Knowledge and understanding of the world (designing and making skills).
	Physical development (using tools and materials).
Key early learning goals	Select the tools and techniques they need to shape, assemble and join materials they are using.
	Handle tools, objects, construction and malleable materials safely and with increasing control.
Resources needed/ enhancements to provision	Hole punches, scissors, treasury tags, stapler, paper clips, paper fasteners, rubber bands, pipe-cleaners, string, threads, open-eye needles (plastic ones are the safest).
	Pieces of card, paper, fabric, cellophane, foil, plastic sheeting etc.
	A 'line' suspended across a wall or under a shelf that can be used to display children's mobiles. Coat-hangers can also make effective hanging frames for mobiles.
	Examples of commercially produced items that can be used to demonstrate different joining techniques, e.g. straps and handles attached to bags with metal links, sewn articles, book bindings, curtain rings and hooks.

Preparation	Make sure that children have a wide range of experiences, across all areas of provision, that enable them to practise and develop fine motor skills. Ensure that stocks of the necessary consumable materials are adequate.
Key vocabulary	Through, in, out, under, over, push, pull. Correct names of tools and materials.
Activity content	Trying out tools and comparing their effectiveness on different materials. Experimenting with techniques. Watching the attempts of others (children and adults) to join materials. Evaluating the success of techniques. Handling and, if appropriate, dismantling items, looking closely at the joining techniques used. Attaching different materials together using a range of techniques to create a mobile. Finding a way of hanging their mobile on the display string or coat-hanger.
Adult role	Monitor children's use of materials and replenish stocks when necessary. Allow children time for tactile explorations of the materials before beginning to make the mobiles. Demonstrate skills and model techniques. Talk with children about the range and effectiveness of techniques they have used. Ask open-ended questions to encourage them to learn from 'mistakes' and to select appropriate tools and joining techniques in the future.
Follow-up ideas	Provide materials and tools on a permanent basis. Encourage children to use skills and techniques in different contexts and for a range of purposes, e.g. making models or books, working in the office, building dens in the outdoor area.

Creature features

Children are captivated by 'larger than life' creatures and this activity will offer numerous and diverse learning opportunities, leading children into an imaginary world of monsters and adventures.

Building a car

Creature features

Key areas of learning	Mathematical development (shape, space and measures).
	Knowledge and understanding of the world (designing and making skills).
	Creative development (exploring media and materials, imagination).
Key early learning goals	Use language such as 'circle' or 'bigger' to describe the shape and size of solids and flat shapes.
	Use developing mathematical ideas and methods to solve practical problems.
	Build and construct with a wide range of objects, selecting appropriate resources and adapting their work where necessary.
	Select the tools and techniques they need to shape, assemble and join materials they are using.
	Explore colour, texture, shape, form and space in two or three dimensions.
	Use their imagination in art and design, music, dance, imaginative play and role-play and stories.
Resources needed/ enhancements to provision	Rolled paper (different lengths and widths).
	Card tubes and boxes.
	Corrugated card.
	Sheets of cheap paper or newspaper.
	Plastic yoghurt pots and margarine tubs.
	Dried split peas, shells, corks, plastic bottle tops.
	Scissors, sprung 'snips'.
	Masking tape.
	PVA glue.
	Pictures and posters of dinosaurs, animals, insects and fantasy creatures.
	Clipboards, paper and pencils.
Preparation	Set up small world environments that enable children to explore features of creatures such as dinosaurs, lizards, crocodiles, rhinoceroses, spiders and crabs.
	Provide books (in the book area or on interactive displays) that show illustrations, and describe features, of different creatures.
	Offer children prior opportunities to work on large-scale construction projects using a range of tools, techniques and materials.
	Ensure that there is enough space for children to work on a large scale – it may be appropriate to clear an area of floor space.
Key vocabulary	Mathematical language: big, small, tall, short, long, heavy, round.
	Technical language: cut, tear, roll, bend, wrap, stick, join.
	Descriptive language: spiky, fierce, slimy, sharp, green, muddy.
Activity content	Talking about familiar creatures and their own imaginative ideas.
	Drawing pictures of their imaginary creatures.
	Building on prior technological knowledge to select tools and materials appropriately.
	Experimenting with materials and techniques to find the most effective way of building their creatures, e.g. screwing up paper to 'pad out' the body and attaching this with masking tape, taping two or three paper rolls together and bending them to create a long neck.
	Adding textures to skin, e.g. by sticking split peas to the body surface to create a 'knobbly' appearance or shells to give a scaled effect.
	Developing ideas about the character of the creature as work progresses.

Adult role   Look at books about, and pictures of, different creatures with children. Compare features and habitats.

Encourage children to express their imaginative ideas. Talk about your own ideas. Describe an imaginary creature and ask the children to draw it.

Support children in using tools appropriately and safely.

Help children to construct a strong 'skeleton' structure around which they can build their creature.

Encourage children to work together and share ideas.

Ask questions to stimulate the imagination and challenge thinking, e.g. 'Why has your creature got wings?' 'Why does it need such sharp teeth?' 'Where does it sleep?' 'How will your creature reach the leaves at the top of the trees? Long legs? Long neck? Wings? Strong arms for climbing?' 'What can we use to make its legs? Will the narrow tubes be strong enough?'

Model technical skills and use of key vocabulary.

Follow-up ideas   Paint and decorate the model creatures and create an environment for them to live in. The outdoor area can provide a very real habitat or large, potted plants can help to create a 'jungle' atmosphere inside. With children, build shelters or caves for their creatures to sleep in. Encourage imaginative play and story making using the models.

Use the children's ideas about the diet, habitat, physical features and character of their creatures to create an information book. Photographs, or children's drawings, of the creatures can be used as illustrations.

Share 'monster' stories such as *Where the Wild Things Are* (Maurice Sendak) and *Not Now Bernard* (David McKee) with children.

3 Sand (wet and dry)

Introduction to the area

The sand tray is usually a popular area, attracting young children to spend considerable amounts of time exploring this inexpensive and readily available material.

If there is plenty of space available in the setting, it is advisable to offer two sand areas on a permanent basis, a wet sand area and a dry sand area, as each of these will provide different learning experiences for children. If space is limited, the wet and dry sand provision can be alternated, or one can be positioned inside and the other in the outdoor area. Any outdoor sand trays or pits should be covered securely when not in use to make them inaccessible to cats or other animals and to protect them from adverse weather conditions.

Flooring in the indoor sand area needs to be considered with regard to safety and practicality. Loose sand should be swept up regularly so as not to cause a hazard – children can be encouraged to share responsibility for this task. There should always be enough sand available to enable children to engage in satisfying investigations and it is a good idea to keep a few bags in stock. It is also important to ensure that children are able to work cooperatively and encouraged to talk to each other about their work, and this means providing space all around the tray.

Basic resources

Furniture and storage

- Open-shelving units for easy storage and accessibility. The shelves should be templated for key pieces of equipment.
- Labelled baskets and boxes for 'sets' of equipment.
- Hooks on the wall for items such as dustpans, brushes and plastic kitchen utensils. Make sure that the hooks do not present any safety problems.
- Plastic jars with screw-top lids for storage of gravel and pebbles.

Equipment and materials

- Bags of play sand.
- A selection of coloured sands.
- Deep sand trays at child (standing) height – rectangular or circular, and shallow trays, e.g. large builders' mixing trays and small rectangular trays.
- A rigid, movable shelf to fit across the sand tray – wide enough for children to stand containers on.
- A long-handled sweeping brush, dustpans and brushes.
- Natural objects, such as shells, pebbles, driftwood.
- Varying grades of gravel, pebbles, shells.
- Pans, cake and bun baking tins, plastic cups, saucers, bowls, plates, egg-cups, jugs.
- Spoons (wooden, plastic, metal) of varying sizes.
- Scoops, spades.
- Buckets (varying sizes, some transparent).
- Small world equipment, e.g. jungle and farm animals, Land-Rovers and tractors (see also Chapter 1).

Wet sand

- Trowels, plastic kitchen fish slices.
- Hard hats.
- Moulds (plastic jelly moulds, animal moulds, regular shape moulds).
- Tools for imprinting and pattern making, e.g. plastic pastry cutters, potato mashers, plastic hair combs, clay modelling tools, old training shoes or wellington boots and toy car tyres (tread patterns).
- A collection of buttons.

Dry sand

- Sand wheel.
- Funnels.
- Plastic bottles, some with holes cut into the side at varying levels.
- Plastic tubes, half pipes.
- Sieves, colanders, flour sifters, salt shakers, buckets with holes, slotted spoons.
- Plastic weighing scales or a balance with pans.
- Teapots.
- Containers with lids, e.g. plastic film canisters, biscuit tins.
- Individual shallow trays (for finger mark-making in sand).

What will the children do and learn?

- Explore sand using appropriate senses – touch, hearing, sight.
- Investigate and compare the properties of wet and dry sand.
- Comment on changes that take place when materials are mixed together.
- Identify, and talk about, features of natural objects they handle.
- Explore pattern through mark-making with tools, imprinting and arranging items in wet sand.
- Make hand- and footprints in sand.
- Make letter shapes with fingers or tools in dry and wet sand.
- Make lines and patterns by pouring coloured sand from plastic salt pots.
- Handle equipment with increasing control and develop coordination skills through activities such as pouring sand from one container to another.
- Learn about capacity and volume – filling and emptying, building with wet sand. Use words such as 'full', 'empty' and simple mathematical language to describe size and shape.
- Compare weights and amounts using related vocabulary, e.g. 'heavy', 'light', 'more', 'less'.
- Count how many scoops of sand it takes to fill a container.
- Find ways of moving dry sand from one place to another, e.g. using pipes, tubes.
- Select appropriate tools for a task.
- Play imaginatively, building their own small world environments and making up stories, represent experiences and explore roles, e.g. baking a cake, being a builder.
- Begin to understand how maps work. Use small world buildings in the sand and talk about features of the local area. Make 'roadways' in the sand.
- Explore sound, making their own musical 'shakers' by putting sand, gravel etc. in sealed containers such as plastic film canisters.
- Talk about ideas, make predictions, discuss plans and findings.
- Work cooperatively, e.g. one child holds the bucket as another pours dry sand into it from a jug.

Making the dinner

Display tips

- 'Tactile' numbers – sandpaper (varying grades) numerals displayed at child height and easily accessible.
- Holiday photographs, brought by children, of seaside experiences.
- Posters of crabs, seagulls, seaweed, shells, pebbles, beaches.
- A shell mobile suspended over the sand tray.
- Transparent plastic containers filled with different coloured sands.
- Photographs of builders mixing cement, pictures from builders' merchants' catalogues of trowels, spades, cement mixers, trays, sand bags etc.

Links with other areas of provision

Water

Some resources can be interchangeable e.g. sand/water wheel, jugs, buckets, tubes and pipes. Sand and water areas can be combined for 'seaside' activities and to enable children to experiment and observe changes as sand and water are mixed.

Role-play

A large, shallow sand tray, jugs of water and old wooden bricks make an exciting 'builder's yard' role-play area and will encourage children to mix 'cement' and build walls.

Technology workshop

Children can use recycled materials (e.g. cereal boxes, cardboard tubes) to represent buildings when constructing small world environments.

Focus activities in the sand area

Ice cream parlour

Develop scientific learning in the context of role-play with this ever-popular activity.

Ice cream parlour

Key areas of learning	Knowledge and understanding of the world (exploration and investigation).
	Creative development (imagination, responding to experiences and expressing and communicating ideas).
Key early learning goals	Investigate objects and materials by using all of their senses as appropriate.
	Look closely at similarities, differences, patterns and change.
	Ask questions about why things happen and how things work.
	Use their imagination in art and design, music, dance, imaginative and role-play and stories.
	Respond in a variety of ways to what they see, hear, smell, touch and feel.
Resources needed/ enhancements to provision	Four plastic sundae dishes.
	Long-handled teaspoons.
	Four small plastic jugs.
	Plastic 'squeezy' bottles.
	A large bowl of water.
	Small plastic bowls containing assorted beads, sequins and wooden matchsticks.
Preparation	Give children opportunities to work in both wet and dry sand and talk with them about the differences.
	Discuss with children their experiences of ice creams and sundaes. Show them menus with photographs of ice cream desserts and ask them which they would like to eat. Perhaps take them to a cafe, ice cream parlour or van and allow them to chose and eat an ice cream.
Key vocabulary	Wet, dry, mix, stir, pour, change, different, same.
Activity content	Exploring new materials and equipment.
	Scooping sand and pouring water into their sundae dish and mixing.
	Observing what happens when sand and water are mixed and talking about their observations.
	Handling their sand and water mixture, stirring it with their fingers or hands.
	Experimenting with the consistency of their mixture, anticipating what will happen if more water or sand is added.
	Controlling how wet the mixture is by adding water or sand.
	Mixing beads, matchsticks and sequins into their sand mixture.
	Playing the role of vendor, referring to the menu and asking friends what they would like in their ice cream. Nuts? Strawberry sauce? Cherries?
	Selecting beads, matchsticks and sequins and using these to represent ingredients in their ice creams and to decorate them.
Adult role	Introduce new resources, naming them and talking about their purposes with children.
	Model use of key vocabulary and encourage use of imaginative and descriptive language such as slushy, gloopy, squishy.
	Play alongside the children, taking orders and making ice creams.
	Encourage children to talk about their scientific observations and their ice cream 'recipes'.
	Take photographs of children's ice cream sundaes.
Follow-up ideas	Use photographs of children with their ice cream 'creations' to make menus for a cafe role-play area.
	Offer opportunities for further mixing activities and investigations, e.g. compost and water, cornflour and water (see also chapter 8), compost and sand.

Building sandcastles (wet sand)

Most children will happily spend hours building sandcastles on the beach, becoming deeply engrossed in their play. Recreate that experience with a simple activity that will help to deepen children's mathematical learning.

Building sandcastles (wet sand)

Key areas of learning	Mathematical development (numbers as labels and for counting, calculating, shape, space and measures).
	Physical development (using tools and materials).
Key early learning goals	Say and use number names in order in familiar contexts.
	Count reliably up to 10 everyday objects.
	Recognise numerals 1 to 9.
	In practical activities and discussion begin to use the vocabulary involved in adding and subtracting.
	Use language such as 'greater', 'smaller, 'heavier' or 'lighter' to compare quantities.
	Use language such as 'circle' or 'bigger' to describe the shape and size of solids and flat shapes.
	Handle tools, objects, construction and malleable materials safely and with increasing control.
Resources needed/ enhancements to provision	This activity can take place in a deep sand tray on a stand, or children can work around a shallow builder's tray on the floor. If the latter option is chosen, mats will need to be provided for the children to sit or kneel on.
	Spades, scoops, trowels.
	A range of containers of various sizes and shapes, e.g. yoghurt pots, margarine tubs, plastic buckets, beakers and bowls.
	Flags, numbered 1 to 10. These are easy to make by attaching triangles of paper to wooden 'lolly' sticks.
	Blank flags, pencils.
Preparation	Talk with children about seaside holidays, revisiting beach experiences. Share photographs of beach scenes, and particularly of children building castles in the sand.
	Make sure that numbers 1 to 10 are displayed in the sand area and that children have experience of one-to-one matching.
Key vocabulary	Full, empty, big, small, heavy, light, more, less, flat, round, square, rectangle, triangle, cube, cuboid, cone, cylinder.
	Number names one to ten.
Activity content	Filling and emptying containers.
	Experimenting by making sandcastles with the different 'moulds'.
	Comparing shapes, size and weight.
	Predicting the size or shape of a sandcastle after selecting the mould.
	Matching a sandcastle to its mould.
	Lining up 'castles'.
	Counting sandcastles, developing one-to-one correspondence and reliability.
	Estimating how many castles can fit across the tray.
	Numbering the sandcastles (with flags) randomly or in order.
	Writing numbers on flags.
	Discussing how many more sandcastles are needed to complete a line of five or ten.

Adult role	Model counting skills and the use of mathematical vocabulary. Refer children to number lines when ordering numbers or looking for a particular number. Ask challenging questions such as 'Can you find a mould that will make a bigger sandcastle than this one?' 'How many of the bucket sandcastles do you think it will take to reach the other side of the tray?' 'Were you right?' Make up number rhymes or songs (or modify familiar rhymes) to reinforce children's learning, e.g. 'Ten sandcastles standing on the beach' (to the tune of 'Ten Green Bottles').
Follow-up ideas	Add different containers to the sand tray over a period of days, encouraging further exploration. Provide opportunities for children to explore solid shape in other contexts, e.g. using dough, snow modelling, constructing with wooden blocks. Display the numbers 1 to 10 in other areas of provision and plan opportunities for children to practise and develop counting skills in a purposeful and meaningful context.

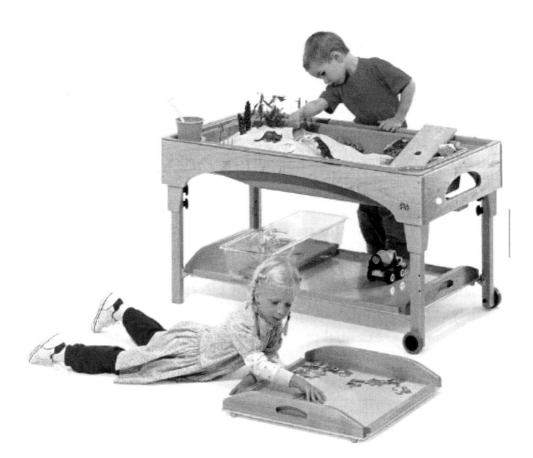

Water

Introduction to the area

With suitable equipment, the water area is particularly rich in opportunities for scientific and mathematical learning, and can also provide a very fertile starting point for imaginative play. Most children are attracted to water and fascinated by its properties. They love to splash in rain puddles, paddle in the sea, wash up in the sink or simply watch as the water disappears down the plughole. Parents will know that even bath time can become an exciting opportunity for learning – a few plastic containers will provide endless hours of fun and exploration, and a collection of small world sea creatures can be all it takes to transform the bath water into an ocean.

The most practical way of offering water in the setting is in a large plastic tray on a stand. These are widely available but vary in design. Some are moulded to incorporate two levels, enabling children to experience different depths of water. Others include channels and 'lock' systems. Transparent trays are also available, some circular and stepped down into the centre.

The water area needs to be situated reasonably near to a tap, as transporting buckets of water over a distance on a daily basis can become very laborious. Ideally, surrounding walls should be tiled and floor coverings should be non-slip. It is not always possible to provide the ideal, but safety must be a priority and a certain amount of water spillage is inevitable. Waterproof aprons should be available, and the children taught that these must be worn at all times during water play. Aprons can serve to limit the number of children working in the water area at any one time; for example, if only four aprons are provided, only four children will be able to access the area.

The outdoor area often offers more space, and here practitioners may be able to provide for water play on a much larger scale. A few trays and buckets at varying levels, connected by plastic drainage pipes and guttering, are guaranteed to inspire young investigators and are relatively inexpensive to purchase. Protective clothing such as splash suits and wellington boots may be advisable for the more adventurous projects.

As in all other areas, children should have access to books that may support or stimulate their learning. There will be practical implications to providing books in close proximity to water but there are ways of guarding against 'splash' damage. A length of perspex attached at right angles across the front of an open shelf will provide protection for the books but will also allow children to refer to pages as they play. It is possible to buy perspex book stands (often used for cookery books) – these also protect the pages while leaving them visible. Books with laminated pages are durable and waterproof and can be easily made using commercially produced pictures and text or photographs of children's own experiences.

Basic resources

Furniture and storage

- Open shelves (on the wall or a free-standing unit). Some templating of equipment on shelves will help to reinforce learning about shape and size, but templates must be sealed and waterproof.
- Plastic storage baskets or boxes for sets of equipment. Baskets are preferable as they allow equipment to dry out quicker.
- Hooks on wall for aprons.

Equipment and materials

- Water tray.
- A stand (some have storage trays incorporated into the frame).
- Waterproof aprons.
- Containers (graded in size, some transparent): cylinders, jugs, plastic bottles, beakers, buckets.
- Siphons, water wheels, funnels, pumps, tubes.
- Slotted spoons, sieves, colanders, tea strainers, plastic bottles with holes made at varying heights.
- Teapots, cups, bowls, spoons, ladles, whisks etc.
- Small world equipment, e.g. sea creatures, boats, people (see also Chapter 1).
- Mechanical or battery-operated boats, fish etc. that move through the water using flippers, propellers or oars.
- Natural materials, such as shells, pebbles, sponges, pumice stones, driftwood, loofahs.
- Watering cans.
- Underwater torches.
- Metal trays and containers, tin foil.
- A range of balls of various sizes and materials.
- Food colouring (to colour water).
- Ice shapes containing materials and items such as sand, glitter, sequins, beads. These can be made in ice cube trays, yoghurt pots, margarine tubs or freezer bags and stored in the icebox of a fridge.
- Tapes of sounds of water, e.g. crashing waves, rain, water going down a plughole, a tap running. (Access to a tape recorder will also be necessary.)
- A mop and bucket.

What will children do and learn?

- Explore the properties of water through appropriate senses – touch, sight and sound.
- Learn about capacity, weight, size and shape.
- Compare and order containers.
- Use vocabulary such as 'full' and 'empty'.
- Compare water levels and begin to understand the concept of measurement, e.g. it takes four cupfuls to fill the bucket.
- Investigate what happens to different materials when they are placed in water, looking at absorbency and water repellence.
- Understand the concept of floating and sinking.
- Sort materials and objects according to whether they float or sink.
- Look at ways of travelling through water, e.g. propellers, sails.
- Learn about how water can be moved.
- Make 'waterways' using half pipes, and experiment with inclines.
- Find out about displacement, e.g. the water spills over the top of the beaker when shells are dropped into it.
- Learn about water freezing and thawing and the effects that temperature changes have on water.
- Talk about observations and ask questions to find out more.
- Experiment and make predictions about what will happen.
- Make suggestions about why things have happened.
- Learn about, and identify features of, creatures and plants that live in water.
- Engage in imaginative play and role-play, such as tea parties.
- Experiment with sound, e.g. dripping water onto tin foil, pouring water into metal containers.
- Listen to, and discriminate between, water sounds.
- Use imaginative language to describe sounds, e.g. 'whoosh', 'tinkle', 'splish'.

Display tips

- Uses of water: photographs of children drinking water, washing hands, brushing teeth, watering plants, swimming etc. These could be displayed on a board or suspended as a mobile.
- Photographs of natural water features, such as waterfalls, rain, rivers, lakes and the sea.
- Photographs of creatures that live in water.
- 'Discovery' displays, e.g. 'We tested lots of materials in the water tray and found that these materials floated/sank.'
- Plastic 'sweet jars' containing materials and objects submerged in water for children to feel and compare, e.g. sponge, chamois leather, bubble wrap, cotton wool.
- Interactive display of small world sailing boats, dinghies, hovercrafts, speedboats, ferries, tugs etc. Where practical, a shallow water tray could be provided. Photographs of different modes of water transport could be displayed on an adjacent board.
- Photographs of children's work on making boats – making, testing, modifying and, finally, the finished design in the water, perhaps carrying a small world person. Lists of materials and techniques used could be included.
- Children's paintings, e.g. bubble prints, 'dribble' pictures (made by using watery paint on a vertical surface), patterns made by blowing paint through drinking straws.

Possible links with other areas of provision

Small world

Small world environments can be built in or around the water tray. For example, an arctic environment could include bubble wrap icebergs, white gravel (to represent ice and snow) and arctic wild life; a pond environment could be created by colouring the water green or brown, adding gravel and providing plastic frogs, tadpoles and pondweed – children could then explore the pond using pond nets.

Technology workshop

If children are able to access materials such as plastic lids and tubs, card and corks they will be able to extend their 'floating/sinking' investigations. They may even make boats or rafts in the technology workshop for use in the water tray.

Role-play – home corner

Washing dolls and their clothes in the indoor or outdoor water area is always a popular activity. Soap, shampoo, face cloths, sponges, towels and combs should be available for such an activity. If possible, a washing line and pegs should also be provided. As well as engaging in role-play, children will be learning about the properties of water and evaporation.

Focus activities in the water area

Juice bar

Introduce children to the concept of measurement through this easy-to-prepare role-play activity.

Juice bar

Key areas of learning	Communication, language and literacy (language for thinking). Mathematical development (numbers as labels and for counting, calculating, shape, space and measures).
Key early learning goals	Use language to imagine and recreate roles and experiences. Count reliably up to 10 everyday objects. In practical activities and discussion begin to use the vocabulary involved in adding and subtracting. Use language such as 'greater', 'smaller', 'heavier' or 'lighter' to compare quantities. Use developing mathematical ideas and methods to solve practical problems.
Resources needed/ enhancements to provision	Three large bowls in the water tray – washing up bowls are ideal. Food colouring: red/pink ('blackcurrant juice'), yellow ('lemonade'), orange ('orange juice'). Board or plank across tray (to serve the cups of 'juice' on). Jugs. Transparent plastic beakers. Waterproof tape. Price list, e.g. half-cup juice, 1p; full cup juice, 2p. Collection of pennies.
Preparation	Fill the three bowls with water and colour each with different food colouring. Mark on the outside of each beaker with a waterproof sticker line to indicate 'half full'. Make sure children have plenty of prior opportunities to fill and empty containers in the water tray.
Key vocabulary	Full, empty, half, pour. Number names one to ten.
Activity content	Taking orders for drinks from friends. Filling and half filling beakers with 'juice' from a jug. Counting how many cups can be filled from a jug full of juice. Counting drinks and pennies.
Adult role	Play alongside children, ordering and paying for drinks and serving drinks. Ask questions such as 'Liam wants one orange juice and two lemonades. How many drinks will he have altogether?', 'How many more cups do you think you will be able to fill from this jug?'
Follow-up ideas	Reinforce children's learning at snack time by marking cups and filling with juice or milk up to the marker. Add food colouring to water on a regular basis – this will make it easier for children to see water levels through transparent containers. Colour water white (powder paint is effective) and create a 'milk float'. Provide a milk crate and plastic 'milk' bottles. Encourage children to fill the bottles with 'milk' before putting them in the crate.

Fishing for numbers

Reinforce children's recognition of numbers through a fun fishing game.

Fishing for numbers

Key areas of learning	Mathematical development (numbers as labels and for counting). Knowledge and understanding of the world (exploration and investigation). Physical development (using tools and materials).
Key early learning goals	Recognise numerals 1 to 9. Ask questions about why things happen and how things work. Handle tools, objects, construction and malleable materials safely and with increasing control.
Resources needed/ enhancements to provision	Nine fish, decorated and numbered 1 to 9. These should be laminated and cut out so that the sealed edge waterproofs the fish. Number lines 1 to 9 (horizontal and vertical) – laminated. Metal paper clips. Small magnets. Fishing rods – pieces of dowel with string attached work well. Sand the ends of rods to make sure that there are no rough edges.
Preparation	Attach a metal paper clip to each fish and tie a magnet onto the end of each fishing line. Place the fish in the water tray. Display number lines in the water area. Display and use numbers in other permanent areas of provision (e.g. house number plaque in the home corner, telephone numbers in the office).
Key vocabulary	Number names one to nine.
Activity content	'Catching' fish randomly. Showing interest in numbers on the fish. Matching caught fish numerals to numerals on number lines. Attempting to catch specific numbers, e.g. in order one to nine, positioning the rod carefully and lowering it with control. Showing interest in, and asking questions about, the way magnets work.
Adult role	Make children aware of safety issues and show them how to use the rods without posing a risk to other children. Support children in recognising numerals, using number names and asking questions such as 'Can you catch the fish with the same number as this one (pointing to number line)?' 'You've caught the number seven fish, can you find number seven on the number line?'
Follow-up ideas	Use six fish (numbered 1 to 6) in the water tray. Ask children to roll a numeral die and to catch the fish that matches the numeral showing on the die. Play 'hopscotch' in the outdoor area. Provide large magnets. Encourage children to explore the nursery, looking for materials that can or cannot be picked up by a magnet.

© Community Playthings Ph: 0800387457.
Used by permission

© Community Playthings Ph: 0800387457.
Used by permission

5 Office and mark-making

Introduction to the area

In all foundation stage settings there should be a permanent area where children know they can find the equipment they need to explore mark-making and begin to record their ideas. Of course this does not mean that children's mark-making and early attempts at writing will be exclusive to this area – opportunities for such activities should be available throughout the setting and suitable equipment included in areas of provision, as outlined in other chapters.

It is important to remember that, in order to develop the physical skills of coordination and manipulation necessary for forming recognisable letters with a pencil, children need appropriate experiences across all areas of provision. These will include handling small equipment, threading, using pegs and pegboards and cutting with scissors. Children will also need opportunities to make marks on a large scale (see also Chapter 11).

When planning opportunities for children to practise and experiment with mark-making and early writing, it can help to consider adults' everyday uses of writing, e.g. taking telephone messages, writing shopping lists, filling in forms. This perspective will inspire lots of practical ideas and will ensure that 'real-life' purposes are being reflected and explored. Adults have a vital role to play in modelling a range of purposes in the setting, and it is important to recognise the value of children's experiences of literacy at home. Sometimes practitioners choose to provide an office area, which, as well as being a resource base for mark-making equipment, can offer children a 'real' context in which to explore writing and other means of communication.

In some settings it may be appropriate to provide portable 'mark-making boxes' or 'office boxes' that can be taken to, and used in, any other area of provision. Ideally, children should have continuous access to the boxes and be able to transport them to their area of play. A permanent office or mark-making area is sometimes used as a central base for the additional boxes. Children certainly need to know where to go to find them if they are to access equipment independently and spontaneously. Adults may also decide to take a mark-making box to an area of provision or a focus activity in order to enhance learning opportunities. Such mark-making provision can be particularly useful in the outdoor area.

A 'themed' office can help to encourage otherwise reluctant children into the office area. The key to success with this approach is to identify an interest, through observation of children, and to develop this interest through the office provision. It could be that a book has been enthusiastically received by children and practitioners decide to 'theme' the office around a key character. For example, the Kipper stories (by Mick Inkpen)

A themed office area

are usually very popular with young children and 'Kipper's office' is sure to inspire. Pictures of Kipper may be added to headed notepaper and address books. Telephone number cards for Kipper's friends could be displayed on the notice board and invitations for Kipper's birthday party provided. Alternatively, practitioners may have noticed a group of children who spend a lot of time in the small world area playing with cars and also enjoy exploring the role of mechanic through garage role-play in the outdoor area. In response to these observations, a 'garage office' may be developed, and equipment such as engine components catalogues, invoice pads, order forms and posters of car models included. Such an approach does not involve a lot of extra work for adults but can have quite a dramatic impact on how the area is used.

A computer is sometimes situated in an area of its own or can be linked to the office area. There are certainly ways in which learning can be enhanced through joint or adjacent provision, and a computer in the context of an office can help to broaden and deepen children's understanding of information communication. However, it is important to remember that, although a computer can be an important tool and support for learning across the curriculum, it is only one way through which children learn about ICT.

Basic resources

The following suggestions relate to an office area that includes a wide range of mark-making tools and materials. Portable mark-making and office equipment can be stored in stacking storage boxes or in 'carry boxes' with handles for easy transportation. Equipment for the portable boxes can be selected from the list of ideas included for the permanent office area.

Furniture and storage

- Low table and chairs. The arrangement of these is important – children need enough table space to work without being cramped and will need easy access to equipment.
- Open-shelf units or wall shelves.
- Plastic 'pencil pots' or small boxes, paper trays, shallow baskets, plastic wall files, letter racks, plastic or wooden storage drawer units – all labelled appropriately.
- Appropriate computer desk or workstation (if a computer is included in the provision) and storage for floppy disks and CDs.

Equipment and materials

- Mark-makers, e.g. pencils (thick and thin), pencil crayons, felt pens, fibre-tip pens, ballpoint pens, dry wipe markers.
- Paper and card – plain, squared, lined, printed forms, notelets, writing pads, invitation pads, memo pads, 'post-it' notes, folded card, postcards, cheque books, greetings cards.
- Envelopes (various sizes).
- Stamps.
- Diaries, calendars, address books, telephone directories.
- Whiteboard.
- Message board.
- Clipboards.
- Disused telephones and answering machines, mobile phones, two-way battery-operated phones or 'walkie-talkies'.
- Glue sticks, sticky tape, treasury tags, paper clips and fasteners, rubber bands, rubbers.
- Rulers.
- Scissors, staplers, hole punches, pencil sharpeners.
- Date stamp.
- Cardboard envelope files, ring binders.
- Postbox.
- Clock.
- Word and phrase bank (e.g. 'Dear', 'From', 'Happy Birthday', children's names).
- Alphabet frieze or poster.
- Waste-paper bin.
- Old computer and keyboard (for free exploration of keyboard and computer purposes in role-play).
- Operational computer, keyboard, printer.

Practitioners may need to introduce some of the equipment suggested only when adult support is available. Children will need to be taught how to use equipment such as scissors and staplers correctly and safely.

What will children do and learn?

- Explore tools and materials, looking closely at and comparing effects.
- Explore stages of mark-making and early writing.
- Represent ideas through marks.
- Understand the difference between drawing and writing.
- Understand that writing communicates meaning.
- Explore a range of purposes for writing.
- Develop the physical skills of control and coordination.
- Learn how to use mark-making tools and office equipment safely and effectively and select appropriately for a task.
- Use correct vocabulary and terminology when referring to equipment and techniques.
- Engage in office role-play taking telephone messages, orders etc.
- Dial telephone numbers, engage in telephone conversations, take turns in speaking and listening.
- Send messages, letters and birthday cards to each other.
- Understand the purpose of the postal system.
- Recognise letters and familiar words.
- Explore and recognise letters on a keyboard.
- Attempt to write their own name and familiar words or type them on a keyboard.
- Print letters, words and labels.
- Begin to link sounds to letters.
- Send and receive e-mails.

Display tips

- A display of greetings cards (e.g. birthdays, festivals), and party invitations alongside photographs of the occasions can help to raise children's awareness of the range of purposes for writing. Cards can be displayed effectively as a mobile hanging from a framework. This type of display has the added advantage of enabling the viewer to look at both sides, and the inside of the card. Parents and carers can be involved in a display of this nature, providing examples from home.
- Photographs of people writing in everyday situations, e.g. signing cheques, making shopping lists, writing letters.
- Annotated examples of children's attempts at writing in the office area.

Possible links with other areas of provision

Sand

A shallow sand tray offers a useful medium for exploring mark-making. Children will use their fingers or other tools to make patterns and letter shapes.

Paint

This area can also provide rich opportunities for mark-making on a large scale with a range of tools.

Role-play

Any role-play area will provide a context in which children can find out about, and experiment with, different 'real-life' purposes for writing, e.g. an appointments diary in a clinic, message pads and shopping lists in a home corner and booking forms in a travel agent's.

Focus activities in the office and mark-making area

Sending postcards

Motivate children to write home and share in their delight when their postcard is delivered to their house. Although this activity has a clear focus on children's writing development, it also offers rich opportunities for talking about different environments and for developing fine motor skills in a meaningful context.

Sending postcards

Key areas of learning	Communication, language and literacy (writing).
	Knowledge and understanding of the world (sense of place).
	Physical development (using tools and materials).
Key early learning goals	Attempt writing for different purposes, using features of different forms, such as lists, stories and instructions.
	Observe, find out about and identify features in the place they live and the natural world.
	Handle tools, objects, construction and malleable materials safely and with increasing control.
Resources needed/ enhancements to provision	Blank postcards. These can be bought from stationers but are often rather small. A4 sheets of card cut in half are a more suitable size and can be made to look realistic by sticking a printed sheet on one side (address lines, stamp space etc.).
	A range of holiday brochures.
	Scissors.
	Glue sticks.
	Stamps.
	Suitable mark-making tools.
	A record of children's home addresses.
	Examples of written postcards.
Preparation	This activity is most effective if planned alongside a holiday role-play. Talk with children about holidays, encouraging them to share their own experiences.
	Find out where the nearest postbox is and plan a safe route from the setting.
	Organise appropriate staffing ratios for group visits to the postbox.
	Inform parents of the purposes of the activity.
Key vocabulary	Write, read, address, words, letters, to, from, stamp, post, postbox, deliver.
Activity content	Looking through holiday brochures.
	Talking about features of different destinations and comparing these with the local environment.
	Selecting pictures of places to cut out and stick onto the front of their postcard.
	Making their own marks to write messages to families.
	Talking about their own address – number of house, name of street etc.
	Sticking the stamp in the correct position on the postcard.
	Posting their own postcard in the postbox (in small groups).
Adult role	Talk about postcard examples and read these to children.
	Model writing skills.
	After discussion with children, write their address on the postcard.
Follow-up ideas	Encourage children and families to send postcards to the setting when they go on holiday. Make a collection of these in a scrapbook or on a wall display.
	Look at the different kinds of mail that are delivered by post, e.g. letters, bills, invitations, appointment cards.
	Visit a post office with children or arrange for a post office worker to visit the setting.

Checking my messages

Message boxes

Encourage children to use writing to communicate with their friends by setting up a system of personal message boxes in the office.

Message boxes

Key areas of learning	Personal, social and emotional development (making relationships). Communication, language and literacy (reading, writing).
Key early learning goals	Form good relationships with adults and peers. Know that print carries meaning and, in English, is read from left to right and top to bottom. Attempt writing for different purposes, using features of different forms such as lists, stories and instructions. Write their own names and other things, such as labels and captions, and begin to form simple sentences, sometimes using punctuation.
Resources needed/ enhancements to provision	A message box for each child and member of staff – this could be a covered cardboard box or a plastic container. Fabric storage pockets can also be used. Message pads, writing paper, envelopes. Mark-making tools. Children's name cards.

Preparation	Identify the message boxes with children's names and symbols or pictures that will be meaningful to them. The same picture that is used to label their coat peg could be used on their message box. Display the boxes in a place in the office area that is easily accessible to children. Plan adult support in the office during the introductory period. Prepare some photocopiable messages that can be sent from staff to children, e.g. 'Dear . . . , please can you water the plants today? From . . . '
Key vocabulary	Write, read, to, from, dear, word, letter, name, envelope.
Activity content	Drawing pictures for friends. Making marks to communicate meaning. Reading back their own marks. Signing messages with their own name. Attempting to write other children's names. Finding the correct box to put their message in. Checking their own box for messages. Attempting to read messages from friends and staff. Responding to messages.
Adult role	Explain to children the purpose of the message boxes and show them how to use the system. Send messages to children. Read messages to children. Encourage children to read their marks to each other.
Follow-up ideas	Encourage parents and carers to use the message boxes when distributing party invitations. Continue to send children messages and plan regular time slots for adults to work in the office supporting children in sending messages to each other. Be aware of the opportunities for making links between areas of provision through the message box system, e.g. sending an appointment card for a child at the role-play clinic. Support children in sending e-mail messages to their friends.

6 Book area

Introduction to the area

For adults, reading often plays a part in the 'unwinding' routine after a busy day. Many of us enjoy recreational reading but, for the experience to be totally pleasurable and relaxing, we need to feel warm and comfortable and often choose to curl up with a book in an armchair or, perhaps, in bed. Likewise, we need to provide an environment in the setting where children can relax with books, an area where they want to spend time browsing and indulging in books.

Careful consideration must be given to the positioning of the area and to the furniture provided if this relaxed and comfortable 'feel' is to be created. Historically, this area has often been referred to as the 'book *corner*' and, although it does not have to be situated in a corner, being partly enclosed by walls can certainly be conducive to a 'cosy' atmosphere. An area can be sectioned off using screens or storage units, and it is important to select a quiet position away from distractions and 'thoroughfares'. The area should be carpeted, or covered with a rug, and seating for children and adults should be comfortable.

Children will not always want to spend long periods of time in the book area. The range of books provided in this area can also serve as a central resource base that can be used by adults and children to support learning in other areas of provision. A child playing with dinosaurs in the sand may access the book area when looking for information about dinosaurs or may choose to refer to the story of 'The Three Bears' during role-play in the home corner. Of course, the book area will not be the only place in the setting where books are in evidence – appropriate fiction and non-fiction books provided alongside interactive displays and in other areas of provision (including the outdoor area) will encourage children to use books spontaneously and independently. Recipe books and catalogues in the home corner, road maps and atlases in the construction area and instruction books in the technology workshop all offer children a real purpose for reading and reflect everyday uses of literacy.

As in all areas of provision, it is important to provide high quality resources. Books that are torn, or have pages missing, are not going to engage or inspire children. There is a wealth of good children's literature on the market and it is worth a browse around a well-stocked bookshop before making any decisions. When selecting books, it is important to think about how positive attitudes towards racial, religious and cultural diversity, disability and gender issues are being promoted. Dual language books are available from bookshops, and it may be possible to arrange for bilingual parents or staff to share stories with children in their mother tongue. A range of formats and illustration styles should be provided and books always displayed attractively.

Making links with the local library can help to give children a broader experience of books and introduce them to the habit of borrowing books. Parents and carers can be invited on these visits and perhaps a rota of support drawn up. Children will enjoy choosing books to take back to their book area and sometimes librarians will be happy to read stories with groups in the library.

Basic resources

Furniture and storage

- Comfortable seating, e.g. large floor cushions, beanbags, sofa, upholstered chairs.
- Suitable storage for books, e.g. wall racks, open-shelf units, wooden 'kinder boxes'.
- A magazine rack for catalogues, brochures and comics.
- A small, low table for the listening centre (positioned near to a plug socket). A storage tray or unit for audiotapes.
- Bags or boxes for the storage of story props relating to particular books. Hooks on the wall for story bags.
- Storage for puppets, e.g. wooden paper towel holders (attached to shelf or table) for glove puppets or a wooden 'mug tree' for finger puppets.

Equipment and materials

- A range of fiction (including traditional and modern stories) and non-fiction books and other reading material.
- Children's made books.
- Audiotapes or CDs: stories (with appropriate book), songs and rhymes, blank tapes, environmental 'sounds' tapes.
- A listening centre.
- Glove and finger puppets, puppet theatre.
- Other story 'props', e.g. pictures, soft toy characters, objects related to particular stories.
- Lengths of fabric, dressing-up clothes.
- Mark-making tools, blank paper, blank made books.

What will children do and learn?

- Select books randomly or with purpose.
- Enjoy, and have favourite, books.
- Share books with friends.
- Join in with rhymes, songs and poems.
- Learn about the basic conventions of books, e.g. be familiar with terms such as 'front' and 'back' of a book, turn pages starting at the front, understand that, in English, print is read from left to right and top to bottom.
- Understand that print carries meaning and that books can be a source of information.
- Use picture clues to find out information and retell familiar stories through pictures.
- Talk about key characters and events in stories.
- Take on the role of key characters.
- Sequence events in stories.
- Predict endings to stories.
- Talk about favourite authors and illustrators.
- Make up their own stories.
- Tell, and record on audiotape, stories.
- Listen to stories on audiotape or CD, following the story in the book.
- Using mark-making equipment, begin to record ideas and produce their own books.
- Begin to recognise some key words.

Display tips

- Carpet tiles attached to walls, boards or cupboard doors provide an effective surface for interactive 'storyboards'. Pictures of story characters and events, laminated and with hoop and loop fastening tape attached to the back, will 'stick' easily to the carpet and will encourage children to retell familiar stories.

- A focus book display can provide a point of interest for children as they enter the area. A low table, or deep shelf, will provide a suitable surface. The display could include a copy of the focus book (fiction or non-fiction), small world equipment or puppets related to the contents, a photograph of the author or illustrator, posters, an audiotape. With an information book about, for example, plants and flowers, a houseplant and magnifying glass could be provided. Practitioners may decide to share the focus book with children at the beginning of the week and leave it on the display for the rest of the week. It may also be possible to arrange for children to take the book, and props, home for a night, perhaps in a story bag or box.

Possible links with other areas of provision

Role-play

In both the indoor and outdoor areas children will relish the opportunity to recreate parts of their favourite stories and develop story ideas of their own. The home corner can become the venue for Kipper's birthday party or the nursery garden a starting point for a search for Billy's Beetle (both ideas inspired by stories by Mick Inkpen). The book area itself can be developed into a role-play area to support children's interests in books, e.g. the provision of a blanket or old curtain draped over a frame in the area to create a 'cave', a bed and a battery-powered lantern can be all it takes for children to 'become' Big Bear and Little Bear from the story *Can't You Sleep Little Bear?* by Martin Waddell.

Technology workshop

Children can explore how books 'work' by looking at, and making their own 'zigzag' picture books or pop-up books.

Computer (see Chapter 5)

With access to a digital camera, children can produce books about their own experiences and interests almost instantly. Documentation of activities through photographs with text added enables children to 'revisit' experiences; for example, a trip to the local carnival, a visit from the dentist to the setting, baking a cake, observing snails in the outdoor area over a period of time. Photographs of children's imaginative play, and their scribed comments and story ideas, can be used to produce fiction books – always remember to credit children as authors, photographers or illustrators. Software such as talking books can offer another dimension to children's learning about books and stories, and suitable websites or encyclopaedias on CD-ROM can provide a valuable source of information.

Focus activities in the book area

'Whatever next?'

Make up a box of props to enhance children's enjoyment of this popular story.

'Whatever next?'

Key areas of learning	Communication, language and literacy (language for communication, reading).
	Creative development (imagination).
Key early learning goals	Listen with enjoyment and respond to stories, songs and other music, rhymes and poems, and make up their own stories, songs, rhymes and poems.
	Retell narratives in the correct sequence, drawing on the language patterns of stories.
	Use their imagination in art and design, music, dance, imaginative play, role-play and stories.
Resources needed/ enhancements to provision	A large cardboard box containing:
	A copy of the book *Whatever Next* by Jill Murphy.
	A soft toy bear and owl.
	A pair of wellington boots.
	A colander.
	A picnic set and rug.
Preparation	Read the story *Whatever Next* with children, using the props.
Key vocabulary	Bear, owl, moon, space, chimney.
	First, then, next, after, before.
Activity content	Exploring the props and relating them to characters and events in the story.
	Looking through the book, reading the pictures and retelling the story using the props.
	Engaging in role-play and 'acting out' the story, dressing up in the boots and colander 'helmet'.
	Imagining, and talking about, situations such as having a picnic on the moon.
	Using the cardboard box to go on rocket trips to imaginary places, introducing storylines of their own into their play.
Adult role	If appropriate, play alongside children, taking on character roles or reading the story as they act it out.
	Support children's own story ideas by adding extra props as required.
Follow-up ideas	Build a spaceship and lunar landscape in the outdoor area.
	Prepare picnic food and hold a 'moon picnic' for children and their teddy bears.
	Make a video recording of children's play and narrate the *Whatever Next* story to go with the film. Share the video recording of the *Whatever Next* story with other children.
	Encourage children to use one object to represent another in their play (as the bear used the colander to represent a helmet in the story).

The story box

Inspire children's imaginative play and encourage them to make up their own stories from a very simple starting point.

The story box

Key areas of learning	Personal, social and emotional development (dispositions and attitudes).
	Creative development (imagination, responding to experiences and expressing and communicating ideas).
Key early learning goals	Continue to be interested, excited and motivated to learn.
	Be confident to try new activities, initiate ideas and speak in a familiar group.
	Use their imagination in art and design, music, dance, imaginative play, role-play and stories.
	Express and communicate their ideas, thoughts and feelings by using a widening range of materials, suitable tools, imaginative play, role-play, movement, designing and making, and a variety of songs and musical instruments.
Resources needed/ enhancements to provision	A 'story box' – a covered and decorated shoebox is ideal.
	Contents – these should be as 'open-ended' as possible, e.g. a length of fabric, a natural object such as an interesting shell or stone, a decorated wooden box.
	A designated place in the book area where the 'story box' is kept permanently, e.g. on a display table or shelf.
	A camera.
	A clipboard, paper and pen.
Preparation	Tell children 'made up' stories using props and the children's own experiences for inspiration. Encourage them to contribute their own ideas to the stories.
	Offer plenty of opportunities for imaginative play and role-play.
Key vocabulary	Story, pretend, next, then.
	Who? When? Why? What? How?
Activity content	Anticipating what might be in the box. Gently shaking the box for 'sound' clues.
	Opening the box and taking out the items, one at a time.
	Looking at and handling the items.
	Describing the items.
	Suggesting the significance of items and making links between them.
	Using items to represent other objects in their play.
	Introducing a narrative into their imaginative play.
	Discussing and negotiating themes in imaginative play or storylines.
	Revisiting and developing ideas over a period of time.
Adult role	Introduce the story box and ask open questions to extend and challenge thinking.
	Take photographs of children's play and scribe their imaginative and story ideas.
	Be prepared to provide additional resources to enhance and support children's imaginative ideas as play progresses.
Follow-up ideas	Make the story box items available over a period of time to allow for the development of ideas.
	Introduce new story box items periodically.
	Summarise children's ideas and retell their 'story' at story time.
	Use photographs and scribed comments to compile a storybook.
	Keep this book in the book area and share it with children, encouraging them to talk about their ideas and experiences.

Role-play

Introduction to the area

Children need to be able to make links in their learning, bridging gaps between the familiar and the unfamiliar and extending or reinforcing learning in other contexts. They will use their own experiences as a starting point for investigating 'real life' in a secure environment. Imaginative play provides children with the opportunity to represent the world around them and to explore a variety of roles, relationships and cultural traditions. In any well-planned role-play area, the possibilities for learning in the area of social and emotional development are abundant.

But imaginative play and role-play must also be valued by practitioners for the context they offer for learning across the whole curriculum. Opportunities for creative and language development are rich as children communicate their experiences and ideas. Purposes for writing (see also Chapter 5) can be explored through role-play and the development of mathematical ideas used to solve practical problems in a 'real' situation. The home corner can be a particularly appropriate place in which children's awareness of time is raised and their understanding of past and present events developed. A range of role-play experiences will also offer a wide variety of opportunities for children to talk and find out about everyday uses of ICT, e.g. bar code scanners and swipe cash cards in a shop; telephones, washing machines (with programme dials), and televisions with remote controls in the home corner; a 'walkie-talkie' or plug-in baby monitor intercom system for ordering meals at a fast food outlet.

Where space allows, teams often provide a permanent home corner and an additional role-play area whose focus is changed regularly. The out-door area should be used to its full potential and can often offer an extra dimension to role-play; for example, a camp (tents made from old curtains draped over wooden frames) set up in the open air will give children a much more authentic experience than the same equipment provided in a hall. When setting up a role-play area, practitioners need look no further than everyday life experiences for inspiration – supermarkets, libraries, clinics, veterinary surgeries and garden centres are all good starting points. It is important to remember that children's personal experiences will vary and to guard against making assumptions about their understanding of the world around them. The introduction of a new role-play area can be planned to coincide with an appropriate outside visit (e.g. a walk along the local high street when setting up a shop) or visitor to the setting (e.g. a health visitor for clinic role-play) – the experiences will complement each other, leading to enriched play and deeper understanding.

Practitioners should always be aware of children's interests and their observations of children's play will often lead to the setting up of a particular role-play area. If a group of children are spending a lot of time with a train set in the small world area, adults may decide to construct a railway station and ticket office enabling them to explore and extend their ideas in a different context. Favourite stories can also provide an exciting starting point for role-play (see Chapter 6). Children should be offered opportunities to contribute, practically and conceptually, to the setting up of new areas and, where practical, be encouraged to build role-play areas to support their play and ideas independently.

The adult role in supporting children's imaginative play and role-play is diverse and success depends on observation and sensitive intervention. The provision of appropriate materials and equipment is essential. These will include purpose-built furniture and other commercially produced equipment, but children also need access to more 'open-ended' resources, such as lengths of fabric and large cardboard boxes, in order to create their own environments. After a period of observation, an adult may decide to become involved in the children's play or may be invited to join in. Such interaction can be very valuable and the modelling of skills (such as following a recipe or appropriate use of the cooker or washing machine in the home corner) is an important part of the role. Sometimes, however, it is right to stand back as children engage with each other and the immediate environment, and allow them to get on with the serious business of making sense of their world without interruption from adults.

Basic resources

The following lists relate to the setting up of a home role-play area. Suggestions for resourcing other role-play areas are included on page 59.

Furniture and storage

A trolley suitable for the storage of 'dressing-up' clothes.

Kitchen/dining area

- 'Room divider' screens.
- Units: cupboards, sink, washing machine, cooker, fridge/freezer.
- A low table, four chairs, baby's high chair.
- Wall shelves (or unit tops) templated for pans, plates etc. Templates can also be applied to vertical surfaces such as screens, walls or the back of a dresser, with corresponding utensils hung on hooks.
- A vegetable rack (or similar storage system) for play food.

Sitting room

- An upholstered sofa and chairs.
- A low 'coffee' table.
- A television/video unit.

Bedroom with hand basin

- A child-sized bed with mattress.
- A baby's cot.
- A washbasin unit.
- A dressing table.
- A jewellery box.

Equipment and materials

- A selection of 'dressing-up' clothes reflecting a range of cultures and occupations and suitable for different social occasions and weather conditions. Bags, purses.
- A variety of dolls representing both males and females and reflecting ethnic diversity.

Kitchen/dining area

- Plates, bowls, cups, saucers, knives, forks, spoons (in coloured sets).
- Play food, recycled packaging such as cereal boxes, gravy granule drums. (Always ensure that recycled materials are safe to use, e.g. check that there are no sharp edges and that containers are empty and clean.)
- Wooden spoons, chopsticks, spaghetti spoons, ladles, slotted spoons, fish slices, rolling pin, biscuit cutters.
- Baby bottles, feeder cups, bowls and spoons, bibs.
- Microwave oven.
- Kettle, a teapot.
- Toaster.
- Apron, oven gloves, rubber gloves.
- Washing-up bowl, dishcloth, pan scrub, washing-up brush, tea towel.
- Salt and pepper pots (plastic).
- Saucepans, frying pan, wok, baking tins.
- Recipe cards/books (reflecting a range of cultures).
- Wall clock, egg timer.
- Washing powder (empty box).
- Washing-up liquid (empty plastic bottle).
- Clothes airer, washing line, pegs.
- Laundry basket.
- Iron, ironing board.
- Dustpan and brush.
- Bucket.
- Vacuum cleaner.

© Community Playthings Ph: 0800387457.
Used by permission

Sitting room

- Magazine rack – television magazines, children's comics, catalogues.
- Television, video recorder or radio, remote control.
- Telephones, directories, address books.
- Notepads, writing paper, cards, pencils, pens.
- Clock.
- Imitation fire, mantelpiece, fireguard.
- Photographs in frames (unbreakable), photograph albums.

Bedroom

- Pillow and bedding.
- Slippers.
- Soft toys.
- Cushions/beanbags.
- Favourite storybooks.
- Jewellery.
- Alarm clock.
- Water bottle.
- Flannel, toothbrush, hand towel, soap (empty dispenser).
- Full-length mirrors.

Resource ideas for other role-play areas

Doctors' surgery/clinic

- Reception area.
- Telephone, computer monitor and keyboard, diary/appointments book, appointment cards, pens and pencils, index card box.
- Waiting area with chairs, low table, magazines, toy box.
- Appropriate doctor and nurse clothing.
- Eye test chart, height measure, weighing scales.
- Baby mat, nappies.
- Stethoscope.
- Bed, chair, desk.
- Charts, forms, clipboard.
- 'Good health' leaflets and posters.

Airport

An aeroplane and runway could be constructed in the outdoor area and play linked to the indoor airport area.

- 'Lounge' area – comfortable seating, low tables, self-service food bar or kiosk.
- 'Check-in' area – conveyor belt, computer screen, luggage weighing point.
- Walk-through scanner.
- Currency exchange.
- Information desk, computer screen showing schedules.
- Car rental point.
- Suitcases, hand luggage, luggage labels.
- Passports, tickets.

Library

The book area could be used as the site for library role-play, or could be linked to the library counter area and used for book stock and browsing.

- Counter with computer monitor and keyboard, telephone, 'pen' scanners.
- Bank postcards (for ordering books), index card files.
- Range of books (marked with 'bar codes') on shelves and in boxes.
- Bookmarks.
- Magazines and newspapers.
- Comfortable seating.
- Leaflets and posters: author information, places of local interest, bus and train timetables, forthcoming festivals and fairs.

Estate agent

The estate agent's office could be linked to the home corner, the latter area being used to 'sell'.

- Desk, computer monitor and keyboard.
- Sofa or upholstered chairs.
- Diary/appointments book.
- Street map book of local area.
- Street maps and aerial photographs on wall.
- Photographs and details of individual houses.
- Camera.
- Tape measure.
- Clipboard, plain paper, forms (house details to be added), pens and pencils.
- 'For sale' signs.
- Open/closed sign.

Shoe shop

- Shoes, slippers and boots, in a range of sizes and styles.
- Shoe- and boot boxes.
- Foot measures.
- Foot templates (graded in size) on card or floor for foot measurement and matching feet to shoes.
- Chairs and footstools.
- Full-length or foot mirror.
- Posters and pictures of shoes and feet.
- Cash till.
- Open/closed sign.

Cafe or restaurant

- Menus, menu board (chalkboard or whiteboard).
- Plastic trays.
- Plates, cups, bowls, plastic glasses, cutlery, play food.
- Order pads, pens and pencils.
- Aprons.
- Tablecloths, serviettes, flowers in unbreakable vases.
- Open/closed sign.
- Cash till.
- Telephone.

Cinema or theatre

- Box office with cash till, telephone, seating plan.
- Tickets.
- Popcorn stall, ice-cream trolley.
- Torches.
- Programmes, 'trailer' posters.
- Stage or screen with curtains.
- Benches or row of chairs.

Garden centre

The outdoor area is an ideal location for a 'garden centre'.

- Plant pots, plastic troughs, watering cans, seed trays.
- Trolleys.
- Spades and trowels.
- Buckets containing gravel, sand, compost.
- Seedlings (children can be involved in growing these), imitation plants.
- Cash till.

Supermarket

- Cash till/card swipe machine.
- Conveyor belt.
- Receipts, money.
- Shopping list pads, pens and pencils.
- Handbags, purses.
- Shopping trolleys, baskets, paper bags.
- Shelves, empty packets and boxes.
- Open/closed sign.

What will children do and learn?

- Explore equipment.
- Draw on personal experience to use equipment appropriately.
- Use gestures, facial expressions and actions to communicate.
- Use talk to link and explain ideas.
- Recall and represent personal experiences.
- Further explore experiences.
- Share ideas and ask questions.
- Use objects to represent other things.
- Imitate adults and explore roles.
- Negotiate roles.
- Play cooperatively, developing ideas with others.
- Use language to recreate roles.
- Explore feelings and relationships.
- Express anxieties and fears.
- Imagine situations.
- Engage in 'fantasy' play and begin to make stories.
- Recall familiar stories, recreating key characters and sequencing events.
- Change or extend familiar stories through play.
- Explore literacy and numeracy in a 'real' context.

Display tips

- An interactive 'lock and key' display on a vertical surface in, or near to, the home corner will enable children to experiment with different types of door security/opening systems, e.g. door bolts and chains, door handles and knobs, hinges, locks and keys.

- A food-packaging display using familiar labels and logos. Photographs of the foods could be displayed alongside the labels or could be matched to the labels by children.

- Photographs from magazines of adults and children showing a range of expressions and emotions can help to raise awareness of, and promote discussion about, feelings. Role-play can be a very powerful context in which to explore feelings and emotions, and photographs, or stylised 'feelings' faces, can help to develop the language needed to express these.

- Appropriate 'real-life' photographs alongside photographs of children engaging in imaginative and role-play, e.g. photographs of a Royal Mail van outside a post office and a child emptying the postbox in the nursery.

- Story displays related to children's role-play, e.g. sequenced pictures and captions from *The Tiger Who Came to Tea* (by Judith Kerr) as the children explore this story in the home corner.

Possible links with other areas of provision

Malleable materials

Children will want to bring dough into the home corner and to use the cooker to 'bake' their dough cakes and biscuits. This activity shows imagination and an understanding of what is involved in producing cakes and, if they are allowed to pursue this interest, children's explorations will be contextual and meaningful. With adult support, there will be further opportunities for extending learning. Rather than separating the two areas completely, practitioners could think about providing some shared resources, such as bun tins, wooden spoons and mixing bowls. The practical implications of moving dough from one area to another can usually be addressed successfully with some creative organisation. If the malleable materials work area is positioned close to the cooker in the home corner, children will not need to transport dough over long distances and are less likely to leave a trail of dough crumbs on the floor. Sometimes the home corner kitchen is used as a base for preparing the dough with children and the recipe is permanently displayed on the wall. If it is not possible to link the two areas physically, resources can be duplicated so that children have the necessary equipment in the malleable materials area to explore their interest in food preparation.

Small world

Through imaginative play in small world environments, children can revisit ideas and interests explored in role-play areas. For example, the provision of a doll's house (with dolls and furniture), in addition to a home corner, will enable children to develop further their understanding of the functions of different rooms and equipment, and of roles and domestic routines. Most role-play can be reflected in small world environments and the latter sometimes offer opportunities for extension of ideas, e.g. a post office is a popular choice as a role-play area and enables children to explore aspects of communication in a 'real' context. A small world town set up on a large shallow tray and including a post office, postboxes, roads, numbered houses and a post office van can also enable children to find out more about the collection and delivery of post.

Technology workshop

With access to the materials and equipment available in a well-stocked technology workshop, children will be able to create their own role-play 'props'; for example, using cereal boxes as supports and paper art straws as a 'rack', they could make a barbecue to enhance 'camping' role-play in the indoor or outdoor areas.

Focus activities in role-play areas

Introducing a pet (home corner)

Encourage children to explore and express their own thoughts and feelings, and to develop a sense of responsibility as they care for the 'nursery pet'.

Introducing a pet (home corner)

Key areas of learning	Personal, social and emotional development (dispositions and attitudes, self-confidence and self-esteem).
	Communication, language and literacy (language for thinking).
Key early learning goals	Continue to be interested, excited and motivated to learn.
	Have a developing awareness of their own needs, views and feelings and be sensitive to the needs, views and feelings of others.
	Use talk to organise, sequence and clarify thinking, ideas, feelings and events.
Resources needed/ enhancements to provision	Soft toy (dog or cat).
	Pet basket and blanket.
	Pet carrier.
	Plastic pet food and water bowl.
	Pet food boxes (empty).
	Pet 'toys' (e.g. rubber ball, soft toy).
	Pet brush.
Preparation	Talk with children about their own needs (e.g. security, food, warmth, sleep) and how these are met in the setting and at home.
	Encourage children to talk about their own pets and how they care for them.
Key vocabulary	Dog/cat, basket, blanket, food, water, brush.
Activity content	Holding, stroking and cuddling the new 'pet'.
	Agreeing a name for the pet.
	Discussing, and finding, a suitable place in the home corner for the pet basket.
	Empathising with the new pet's feelings and showing awareness of its needs.
	Reassuring the pet in its new home and explaining routines.
	Taking turns in feeding and brushing the pet.
	Taking responsibility for regular feeding times.
	Negotiating care roles.
	Including the pet in imaginative play and role-play that takes place in the home corner.
	Looking after the pet when it is taken out of the home corner.
Adult role	Introduce the new 'pet' sensitively, giving children responsibility for its welfare.
	Make sure that children are familiar with the names and purposes of pet care equipment.
	Support children's ideas (e.g. if they decide to take the pet for a walk, it might be appropriate to provide a collar and lead after discussions about safety).
Follow-up ideas	Encourage children, in turn, to take the pet home for a night and to look after it. Make time the next day for the child to share experiences with others.
	Set up a veterinary practice role-play area and encourage children to visit with their new pet. If possible, arrange for a vet to visit and talk to the children about care of animals.
	Collect photographs of children's own pets and compile a book including children's comments.
	Encourage problem-solving activities, e.g. 'Can you make a kennel in the outdoor area big enough for our pet to lie down in and waterproof so that he can stay dry in the rain?'

Back in time

Raise children's awareness of their own 'history' and developmental changes through role-play.

Back in time

Key areas of learning	Communication, language and literacy (language for thinking). Knowledge and understanding of the world (sense of time).
Key early learning goals	Use language to recreate roles and experiences. Find out about past and present events in their own lives, and those of their families and other people they know.
Resources needed/ enhancements to provision	Baby and toddler dolls. Baby equipment, e.g. clothes, bottles, food packets, changing mat, nappies, buggy, cot, high chair. Dressing-up clothes to suit different ages. Books and toys suitable for babies, toddlers and older children. Photograph albums showing children at various stages of development and with different generations of family. Age birthday cards, birthday cake with candles.
Preparation	Ask parents to provide photographs of children at different developmental stages and collect photographs of experiences in the setting over time. Compile the photograph albums.
Key vocabulary	Now, then, baby, grow, crawl, walk, talk, young, old.
Activity content	Playing with dolls, exploring the role of adult carer and discussing the needs of their 'babies'. Talking about their own needs and developing independence. Comparing their needs with the needs of a baby. Looking at the developmental changes from birth to adulthood. Sorting toys according to suitability for age groups. Matching clothes to people. Looking through photograph albums. Recalling significant experiences in their own lives, e.g. birthdays, holidays, the birth of a baby in the family. Planning birthday parties.
Adult role	Provide photographs of yourself at different stages in your life. Show these to children and encourage them to ask questions. Engage in role-play, modelling skills such as dressing and bottle-feeding baby dolls. Ask questions such as 'Why couldn't you eat pizza when you were a baby?' 'Your baby can't talk yet, but how does he let you know what he wants?' 'What can you do now that you couldn't do before you came to nursery?'
Follow-up ideas	Ask a parent to come into the setting and talk with the children about their baby's needs. They may be prepared to bath or feed the baby in the setting. Encourage grandparents into the setting, particularly to work with children in the home corner talking about their own lives and the changes they have seen. Visit a clothes or toy shop and look at suitable products for different ages. Plan a food-tasting activity, including smooth and 'lumpy' baby food. Talk about the differences between baby food and the food children eat. Discuss the reasons why babies need special food.

8 Malleable materials

Introduction to the area

Even very young children will often spend considerable lengths of time exploring malleable materials, becoming deeply absorbed in their play and enjoying the sensory experiences offered by such investigations. They may choose to access the area day after day to pursue and develop their learning interests and, although practitioners will want to offer a range of malleable materials over time, provision must be constant enough to allow for revisiting.

A medium such as dough is inexpensive and easy to make. Children can be involved in its preparation (see also Chapter 7) and help to make decisions about texture and colour. It provides a suitable media for modelling and moulding and is malleable enough for young children to manipulate effectively. There are many recipes available, producing a variety of consistencies (see the sample recipe in this chapter). Some need cooking in a pan on a cooker hob or in a microwave oven, but a simple mixture of self-raising flour, water and a little salt will result in a 'stretchy' dough without being cooked. The physical skills developed through squeezing, squashing and using tools will benefit children in many other areas of learning, not least the acquisition of handwriting skills. Dough can be kept in an airtight container in the fridge.

Clay is also a popular choice of material and offers a different tactile experience to dough. It needs to be stored carefully to maintain its quality, and suitable boards should be provided. It is always important to be aware of any skin disorders or allergies when providing materials for children to handle and to watch out for any sensitivity to substances used.

It is inevitable that some dough (or other malleable material) will be dropped on to the floor during a play session and, for this reason, it is a good idea to locate the area on washable flooring.

Children's understanding of form can be deepened through a visit to a local art gallery to look at sculpture. Some settings may even be lucky enough to have access to an outdoor sculpture park. Such a visit would also be likely to motivate children's own creativity and inspire ideas in the malleable materials area.

Basic resources

Furniture and storage

- Round or rectangular table, four chairs.
- Storage baskets for equipment.
- Open shelves (unit or wall-mounted), templated for equipment.
- Airtight boxes and buckets for storage of materials.

Equipment and materials

- Washable aprons.
- Clay boards.
- Flour sifter.
- Modelling tools.
- Cutters (e.g. biscuit cutters), scissors.
- Moulds.
- Items for pattern making and imprinting, e.g. buttons, sequins, beads, coins, textured rolling pins, nail brush, comb, toothbrush, plastic drinking straws, keys.
- Natural objects, e.g. shells, pebbles, tree bark, fir cones.
- Kitchen utensils (make sure that these are safe for children to use), e.g. rolling pins, potato masher, whisk, fish slice, garlic press.
- Weighing scales, balance.
- Baking tins, bun cases.
- Cake boards and decorations.
- Cutlery, bowls, plates, cups.
- Small world equipment such as people, animals and vehicles.
- Dustpan and brush.
- Bars of soft soap or wax (for carving or 'digging').
- Clay. Choose a suitable type for use by children – educational suppliers usually include a range in their catalogues.
- Dough.
- Soap flakes, whisk, warm water (when soap flakes have dissolved, and the mixture has thickened, whisk to required consistency).

Basic dough recipe

The texture and appearance of the dough can be altered by adding, for example, food colouring, glitter or sand. Smells can also be added, e.g. peppermint or vanilla essence, cinnamon, thyme, garlic, perfume.

Ingredients

One cup of water.

One cup of plain flour.

Half a cup of salt.

One tablespoon of cooking oil.

One teaspoon of cream of tartar.

(Double the ingredients to produce larger quantity.)

Method

Mix the ingredients together in a large bowl. Transfer the mixture to a non-stick pan and heat gently, stirring all the time. As the ingredients heat and cook, lumps will disappear and the mixture will form a large ball. (The mixture can also be cooked in a microwave oven.) Remove from the heat and, when cool, knead the dough until smooth.

What will children do and learn?

- Explore materials using their senses as appropriate.
- Be familiar with, and identify, the properties of some materials.
- Develop dexterity through squeezing, pinching, pressing, pulling and tearing and rolling malleable materials.
- Develop control and coordination through handling and using tools.
- Experiment with tools and techniques (e.g. imprinting, making coil and thumb pots, carving).
- Explore solid and flat shape, colour, pattern and texture.
- Show increasing awareness of length, size and weight and use appropriate mathematical language to compare, e.g. 'long', 'longer', 'big', 'small'.
- Develop counting skills and join in number rhymes.
- Use words such as 'soft', 'squashy', 'round' and 'cold' to describe what they see and feel.
- Talk about their own models, explaining ideas and techniques.
- Observe, and talk about, changes that take place when ingredients or materials are mixed together or heated.
- Use malleable materials as a media for representing imaginative ideas.
- Engage in role-play, e.g. baking, shopkeeping.
- Develop imaginative ideas over time.

Display tips

- Recipe chart for dough showing pictures of ingredients, and cup or spoonfuls numbered. The 'method' section could be illustrated with photographs of staff and children preparing dough at each stage.
- Photographic display showing origins of materials such as flour, clay, water.
- Sculpture display including clay plaques and three-dimensional work (a local museum loans service may be able to supply good examples) and posters or photographs of sculptures in stone, marble etc. (e.g. by Henry Moore).
- Word and question display (with annotated photographs) including children's scribed comments during play with malleable materials, e.g. 'Slippy', 'slimy', 'smooth' (exploring clay), 'It gets squelchier when I put water in' (mixing dough ingredients), 'Why is the clay hard now? I can't press it any more!' (handling clay after it has been left out overnight).
- Number rhymes such as 'Five currant buns in a baker's shop', perhaps displayed alongside five dough buns made by the children.

Possible links with other areas of provision

Water/sand areas

Children will be reinforcing such concepts as form, shape and pattern as they work with wet sand, and will be experimenting with mixing materials in the sand and water areas. The large trays used in these areas can also serve as ideal containers for some 'tactile' explorations with malleable materials such as a soapflakes-and-water mixture.

Outdoor area

The outdoor area will offer opportunities for manipulating, and sculpting with, natural materials in a natural environment; for example, snow, clay-based soil, compost and water.

Paint

Patterns imprinted in clay slabs with modelling tools can make effective printing blocks. Children will enjoy producing paint prints of their patterns in different colours. Hardened clay (or baked dough) pots and models can be decorated with paint – a small amount of PVA glue added to the paint will give a shiny, waterproof finish.

Focus activities in the malleable materials area

Cornflour 'gloop'

This mixture will fascinate children and adults alike.

Cornflour 'gloop'

Key areas of learning	Communication, language and literacy (language for communication).
	Knowledge and understanding of the world (exploration and investigation).
Key early learning goals	Extend their vocabulary, exploring the meanings and sounds of new words.
	Investigate objects and materials by using all of their senses as appropriate.
	Look closely at similarities, differences, patterns and change.
Resources needed/ enhancements to provision	Cornflour (one or two packets, depending on the size of the tray). Water (in jug).
	Spoons, forks, plastic spatulas, blunt knives, modelling tools, plastic cutters.
	Large shallow tray. Smaller, individual trays can be used but the opportunities for discussion are more plentiful if a group of children are able to work around the same tray.
	Food colouring.
Preparation	Give children plenty of 'hands on' opportunities to explore a range of malleable materials.
	Ensure that there is plenty of room around the tray so that children can stand and observe if they wish.
	As far as possible, make sure that children's clothes, and surrounding surfaces, are protected.
Key vocabulary	Wet, dry, mix, change, different, same.
	Encourage children to think of, and make up their own, words to describe what they see and feel, e.g. slimy, oozy, squidgy.
Activity content	Pouring or sifting cornflour into the tray and handling it.
	Adding water (coloured with food colouring if required) gradually to the cornflour and mixing the two together using hands and utensils.
	Predicting what will happen if more water or cornflour is added.
	Talking about observations experimenting with language.
	Mark-making and exploring pattern.
	Observing changes in consistency over time.
Adult role	Monitor the consistency of the 'gloop'. When mixed in certain proportions, it has fascinating qualities – it can be cut with a knife or rolled into a ball but, when picked up, runs like liquid through the fingers. The mixture will dry out fairly quickly, becoming more brittle and 'crumby'.
	Work alongside children exploring and experimenting, and modelling use of key vocabulary and descriptive language.
Follow-up ideas	Make the activity available over a number of days, adding water as the mixture dries out.
	Share the experience with parents and carers – this is an activity that is cheap and simple to set up at home.

'Let it snow!'

Try modelling 'snow' people with fondant icing during the winter season.

'Let it snow!'

Key areas of learning	Mathematical development (shape, space and measures).
	Physical development (using tools and materials).
	Creative development (imagination).
Key early learning goals	Use language such as 'circle' or 'bigger' to describe the shape and size of solids and flat shapes.
	Handle tools, objects, construction and malleable materials safely and with increasing control.
	Use their imagination in art and design, music, dance, imaginative play, role-play and stories.
Resources needed/ enhancements to provision	Ready-made roll-out icing.
	Icing sugar.
	Sieves, tea strainers or flour sifters.
	Beads, sequins and small buttons (for decoration).
	Plastic trays (preferably white).
	Photographs or pictures of snow scenes and snow sculptures.
Preparation	Talk with children about their experiences of snow. Try to coincide this activity with snowy weather.
	Knead the icing until it is malleable. It may be too hard for children to manipulate at first.
	This activity can result in icing sugar on the floor – if the flooring is not washable, use a protective cloth.
Key vocabulary	Big, small, round, flat, push, squeeze, knead, poke, pull, roll.
Activity content	Handling the icing – kneading, squeezing, pressing etc.
	Rolling balls of icing and comparing size, e.g. a small ball for the head and a bigger one for the body.
	Modelling snow people using fingers and hands to shape the parts.
	Talking about the different shapes they make.
	Finding ways of 'sticking' the body parts together.
	Decorating the snow people with eyes, noses, buttons etc.
	Using icing sugar (shaken through a sieve or sifter) to create a 'snowfall' on the 'snow' people.
	Talking about imaginative ideas.
Adult role	Work alongside children modelling with the icing and experimenting with ideas.
	Talk with children about their work using key vocabulary and asking questions such as 'Can you make a snowman that is bigger than mine?' 'What do you think will happen if we put the big ball on top of the small one?' 'What shall we use as eyes?'
Follow-up ideas	Display children's snow people. Cardboard boxes carefully arranged and covered in cotton wool or white fabric can be used effectively to produce an Alpine scene.
	Try using packet-mix royal icing (just add water) to create a different consistency. Encourage children to create their own snowy environments using the icing in trays. The icing will dry out overnight – they will then be able to use small world equipment to make footprints and tyre tracks in the 'snow'. This too can be a very messy activity so make sure that clothes and flooring are protected.
	Read the story *The Snowman* (Raymond Briggs) with the children. Encourage them to retell the story through their 'icing' play. This story could also be used as an introduction to the activity.
	Look at the similarities and differences between the icing and real snow.

9 Paint

Introduction to the area

There are practical implications to the setting up of a paint area and, ideally, running water should be readily available so that children can fill up their own water pots and wash up equipment after use. A washable floor surface is also a 'must' and suitable aprons should be provided. Occasionally children are reluctant to engage in paint activities, worried that their clothes may become 'messy' or 'dirty'. It is a good idea to remind parents that some valuable explorations may result in splashes or marks on clothing and that 'best' clothes are not always appropriate. It may also reassure parents to know that the materials used by children are washable.

As in other areas of provision, there should be a balance of adult-led and child-initiated activities. Early years practitioners have an important role to play in supporting children's growing creativity in the paint area, but this does not necessary mean direct intervention. There are times when sensitive interaction in the form of comments, questioning, introducing new equipment or stimuli and modelling of skills and techniques can enhance children's artistic development. At other times children need to have the freedom to explore and express themselves without intervention from adults. The success of both approaches is dependent on the adult recognising when it is the right time to intervene and pitching interactions at a level appropriate to the child's developmental stage. Observation is the key and children's learning interests (e.g. a specific technique or subject matter) should determine the nature of the intervention and any planned focus activities. In order to make choices and pursue interests independently, children need access to a range of stimuli, techniques and materials.

Children should have the opportunity to work on different levels and inclines. Double-sided easels are useful when working in a confined space and allow children a comfortable view of their work, but can lead to frustration as watery paint 'dribbles' down the paper. A flat surface such as a table- or unit top is sometimes more appropriate but chairs are not necessary, as movements will be restricted and brush strokes less free if children are sitting down. If space allows, wall murals or floor paintings (using rolls of lining paper or large sheets) can offer opportunities for collaborative work and enable children to use large arm movements as they apply the paint. They should also be able to engage in two- and three-dimensional projects, and links between the paint area and technology workshop can help to extend opportunities.

There will be times when 'ready-mixed' paint is an appropriate choice, and it can be useful when exploring techniques such as printing or 'splatter' painting. However, children should also have regular and frequent opportunities to mix their own paint. Such experiences allow children to experiment with consistency and colour and may not, initially, even lead to the application of paint to paper. It is not necessary to offer a wide range of colours for mixing – the provision of red, blue and yellow (primary colours) will enable children to produce a rainbow of colours through purple, green and orange (secondary colours). Practitioners may sometimes offer extra materials (to be added to paint) in order to facilitate further investigations into consistency and texture (see 'Equipment and materials').

Sometimes art galleries plan education programmes for young children and offer 'in gallery' sessions when children can explore techniques and materials and experience works of art at first hand. An 'artist in residence' scheme may also be in operation. This will involve an artist working with children and adults, perhaps over a period of time, in the setting. These can be very stimulating experiences and such programmes, if available, should be investigated.

Basic resources

Furniture and storage

- Storage unit or trolley containing trays, baskets, storage boxes. Equipment templates can be applied to tops of units (e.g. for paint pots, palettes).
- Open shelves.
- Square or rectangular table (appropriate height for standing children).
- Cutlery drawers, vertical cutlery drainers (for storage of pencils, brushes, spatulas, rollers etc.).
- Plastic jars or boxes with lids (labelled) for storage of paint and other materials.
- Paper cupboard (open shelves or shallow drawers).

Equipment and materials

- Plain, plastic-coated tablecloth (if required).
- Drying rack.
- Easel(s) with attached trays.
- Paint: powder paints (crimson, vermillion, brilliant yellow, lemon, Prussian blue, brilliant blue, black and white), ready-mixed paints, water-colour blocks.
- Paper: various textures (woodchip wallpaper is inexpensive and offers a coarse texture), colours, weights (including card) and sizes (rectangles of varying proportions).
- Brushes: varying widths, round and flat, e.g. decorators' brushes (assorted sizes), hog bristle, nylon, stencil and foam brushes.
- Rollers, e.g. foam, fabric.

- Water pots (wide base).
- Spatulas.
- Plastic containers for powder paint.
- Palettes (with separate compartments or indentations for mixing colours).
- Resources that act as stimuli, e.g. exotic shells and flowers, feathers, vases (interesting form or pattern), photographs and posters.
- 'Found' objects for making marks with paint and for printing with, e.g. combs, forks, washing-up brushes, pan scrubs, corks, plastic lids.
- Materials to be added to paint, e.g. sand, PVA glue, paste, sawdust, washing-up liquid, flour, glitter.
- Graphite pencils (ranging from 2H to 6B).
- Additional mark-making equipment, such as dry/oil pastels, water-based printing inks, fibre-tipped pens, graphite sticks, chalks, Conté crayons, charcoal and charcoal pencils, may be stored in the paint area.
- Good quality reproductions of works of art, e.g. books, posters and postcards.

What will children do and learn?

- Explore equipment.
- Select appropriate equipment for a task and follow a routine (e.g. paint mixing: water pot, palette, powder paint in containers, brush and spatula).
- Use tools and equipment with increasing control.
- Take responsibility for cleaning own equipment and returning it.
- Mix powder paint with water.
- Mix colours, experimenting with combinations.
- Apply paint to paper randomly, observing effects.
- Explore and experiment with elements such as pattern (random and repeated), line, texture, shape.
- Use appropriate and imaginative language to describe elements of art, e.g. line: 'wiggly', 'curly', 'swirling', 'sharp'.
- Explore a range of painting and printing techniques.
- Use paint to express and represent ideas.
- Engage in mixed-media work.
- Look closely at reproductions of works of art and talk about their observations.
- Make marks on paper to identify own work.

© Community Playthings Ph: 0800387457.
Used by permission

Display tips

- Reproductions and examples of artists' paintings, focusing on, for example, paint techniques, subject matter, styles, time periods, cultures.

- Nursery gallery displaying named and annotated children's work. The content of the gallery should be changed regularly. A 'gallery catalogue' could also be produced (perhaps using a digital camera to reproduce images of children's paintings) for parents and visitors.

- Artefacts (local museums often offer a loans service) and natural forms displayed on white, wooden cuboids (varying sizes and heights). These will provide a point of interest and may inspire children's creative ideas.

- Colour-mixing display illustrating how primary colours can be mixed together to produce secondary colours, i.e. blue + red = purple, blue + yellow = green, yellow + red = orange.

Possible links to other areas of provision

Role-play (home corner)

Reproductions of works of art depicting domestic life in different periods of time and across a range of cultures will add another dimension to children's play. Discussion about the works will help to develop their sense of time and place.

Music and sound

Music can be a powerful stimulus and lead to expressive use of paint. A range of genres can be played on a tape or CD-player in the paint area as children work or in the outdoor area where children may be able to work on a larger scale. Much of Wassily Kandinsky's work was concerned with the analogy between art and music, and reproductions could be displayed in the music and sound area.

Book area

A selection of art postcards (available from gallery shops and some stationers) kept in a 'slot-in' photograph album in the book area can provide hours of interest for children. The postcards (or poster-size reproductions) can also be used as starting points for children's own story ideas.

Focus activities in the paint area

Hand mixing and mono printing

This is a truly 'hands on' activity that will engage children at different developmental stages. Some will become totally absorbed in the sensory experience of mixing paint with their hands and others will be fascinated by, and experiment with, the technique of mono printing.

Hand mixing and mono printing

Key areas of learning	Knowledge and understanding of the world (exploration and investigation).
	Creative development (exploring media and materials).
Key early learning goals	Look closely at similarities, differences, patterns and change.
	Explore colour, texture, shape, form and space in two and three dimensions.
Resources needed/ enhancements to provision	Ready-mixed paint (red, yellow and blue).
	Acrylic boards (one for each child). If tables have smooth, washable surfaces, boards may not be needed.
	Sheets of white paper (suitable quality for printing).
Preparation	Make sure that hand-washing facilities are readily available and that children's clothes are protected.
	Introduce children to colour vocabulary through a range of experiences.
Key vocabulary	Red, yellow, blue, orange, green, purple, change, same, different.
	Language related to line, pattern and shape, e.g. zigzag, wavy, dotty, spotty, big, square, round.
Activity content	Selecting two primary colours and squeezing paint (in separate dollops) on to a board or tabletop.
	Spreading paint with palms of hands and mixing colours together.
	Observing and commenting on colour changes.
	Experimenting with colour mixing.
	Drawing conclusions about formulae for colour mixing from their own experience, e.g. 'When I mix red and yellow together, I always make orange.'
	Using fingers to make marks in paint.
	Refining marks, exploring line, pattern and shape.
	Perhaps using marks to represent objects, ideas or experiences.
	Taking mono-prints from marks in paint by pressing paper onto a board or tabletop and applying even pressure.
	Comparing prints taken at different stages in the mark-making.
Adult role	Support children with skills and routines, e.g. squeezing paint out of the bottle, washing hands and equipment at the end of the activity.
	Demonstrate the technique of mono printing.
	Talk with children about their work, encouraging them to describe their marks and the effects of their colour mixing.
	Ask questions to extend children's thinking, e.g. 'What do you think will happen if we mix some red paint with the yellow?'
Follow-up ideas	Offer children opportunities to try other printing techniques, e.g. vegetable printing, string printing.
	Provide regular opportunities for children to experiment with colour mixing using powder paint, overlapping cellophane 'paddles', adding two food colourings to water or dough.

Printing grid

This collaborative work can be developed over a few days, with all children encouraged to make a contribution.

Printing grid

Key areas of learning	Mathematical development (shape, space and measures).
.	Physical development (using tools and materials).
Key early learning goals	Talk about, recognise and recreate simple patterns.
	Use language such as 'circle' or 'bigger' to describe the shape and size of solids and flat shapes.
	Handle tools, objects, construction and malleable materials safely and with increasing control.
Resources needed/ enhancements to provision	Large-weave plastic webbing from a garden centre (used to support climbing plants).
	Large sheet or sheets of white paper.
	Masking tape.
	Everyday objects to print with, e.g. corks, plastic bottle tops, small boxes (such as packaging for stock cubes), cotton reels, wooden beads (cube). (Alternatively, shapes could be cut into potatoes and these used to print with.)
	Ready-mixed paint in primary colours (e.g. red, blue, yellow).
	Shallow plastic bowls or margarine tubs.
	Pieces of sponge (to fit inside plastic bowls).
Preparation	Plan for children to experience printing randomly with a range of materials.
	Look at grid patterns with children, e.g. using pegs and pegboards.
	Soak sponges in paint (these will be used as paint pads for printing).
	If the webbing has been rolled up, press it so that it lies flat.
	Cover the tabletop, or floor space, with paper and tape it down.
	Then position the webbing on top of the paper and fix it with tape.
Key vocabulary	First, next, last, after, before, same, different, circle, square, triangle, rectangle, big, small, red, blue, yellow.
Activity content	Sorting through everyday objects. Looking closely at, and comparing, objects, looking at shape and size.
	Selecting an object, paint colour and position on the grid.
	Printing with their object in the chosen space.
	Watching the developing pattern as children add their prints, and commenting on their observations.
Adult role	Encourage children to talk about the features of their chosen printing object and the pattern that is emerging on the grid. Ask questions such as 'What shape do you think this bottle top will make when we press it onto the paper?' 'Can you find two prints that are the same shape/colour?' 'Can you find a circle next to a square?' 'Can you make your print next to another yellow shape?' 'Can you make this row match the row above it?' 'Have you noticed anything about the shapes on this row?'
Follow-up ideas	When the grid is complete, and the prints are dry, remove the webbing and display the pattern on the wall at child's eye level.
	Make a set of corresponding pattern cards and encourage children to match shapes to those on the grid. Ask them to create and recreate patterns with the cards.
	Draw a large grid with chalk on tarmac or paving stones in the outdoor area. Ask children to collect natural items, e.g. stones and leaves, and to make a pattern by placing one item in each square.
	Provide blank paper grids, coloured dice, coloured sorting equipment and coloured pencils in the maths area or on an interactive display. Encourage children to make up their own games.

10 Music and sound

Introduction to the area

Music touches all of our everyday lives to differing degrees and is an intrinsic part of contemporary culture. Not only do young children enjoy listening to music, they are also keen to engage in music-making activities. Unlike many adults, most children will experiment confidently and enthusiastically if offered a range of instruments and the freedom to be creative.

Of course, there is a place for adult-led group 'singing' sessions, and learning rhymes and songs plays a valuable role in the preparation for phonics. However, it is important that children enjoy, and see adults modelling, all types of musical activity. Planned sessions will offer a broader experience if they include listening to recorded music and music making. Children should be encouraged to use their own body, as well as commercially produced instruments, in percussion; for example, handclapping, finger clicking. When planning for children's creative development in this area, practitioners should also consider how children's musical experiences link to other expressive art forms, such as movement and dance. Listening games should also be planned into the curriculum. These will help to develop aural awareness and sound discrimination skills.

The provision of a permanent music and sound area can complement group music sessions, allowing children free music play, exploring instruments and revisiting or extending musical ideas. If practical, it would seem appropriate to plan for the more structured sessions to take place in the permanent area. Everyday objects, and resources that enable children to make their own instruments, should also be available. Many of the materials provided in the technology workshop (see Chapter 2) will be suitable for making instruments to beat, shake, pluck or blow. Of course, this will not be the only area in which children are learning about sound. They should be encouraged to listen to, and discriminate between, environmental sounds all around them, both inside and out; for example, the wind in the trees, vehicles, birds, taps running, doors closing, footsteps.

The positioning of a music and sound area will need careful thought. Enthusiastic investigations and performances can be quite loud and it may not be appropriate to place the area next to certain other areas. The outdoor area can offer lots of opportunities for sound exploration and disturbance is usually less of an issue in the open air (see also Chapter 11).

Children may have experienced live musical performances with their families and friends, perhaps at the theatre, local festivals and carnivals or from street performers. It is possible to book musicians to perform in the setting and such a visit can not only broaden and deepen children's appreciation of music, but also be the starting point for other exciting creative and language work. If the fee of a visiting musician is inhibiting, it is worth considering sharing the cost and the experience with another setting.

Basic resources

Furniture and storage

- Unit tops or shelves (templated) for instruments.
- Baskets (natural materials such as wicker or sea grass give another sensory experience) for storage of instruments.
- Mug 'trees' or hooks on the wall to hang instruments such as shakers, bells, made instruments.
- Trays or storage cases for audiotapes.
- Storage boxes for sets of rotated instruments.

Equipment and materials

- A range of instruments; for example, carousel bells, 'sleigh' bells, chime bars, glockenspiels, maracas, calabashes, whistles, recorders, drums (with a variety of beaters), cymbals, castanets, woodblocks and claves, tambourines, rain sticks, zithers, guitars, electronic keyboards and 'footprint' pads.
- Listening centre, headphones, blank and pre-recorded tapes (e.g. environmental sounds, nursery rhymes, songs and instrumental music from different times and cultures).
- Everyday objects, e.g. plastic thimbles, tins.
- Scarves and ribbons (to be used in dance and movement responses to music).
- Song- and rhyme books.
- Paper (plain and wide-lined manuscript), whiteboard, pencils, coloured pens and dry-wipe markers.

Practitioners will probably want to limit the choice of instruments available at any one time, and 'sets' can be offered on a rotational basis. Sets of instruments could be sorted according to how sounds are produced or could offer a range. Some instruments may only be available with adult support.

What will children do and learn?

- Listen to sounds and music.
- Handle and play a variety of instruments.
- Take turns in playing.
- Discriminate between everyday sounds and musical instruments.
- Identify sounds in a piece of recorded music.
- Match sounds to instruments.
- Experiment with instruments, voices and everyday objects, exploring how sounds can be made and changed.
- Begin to organise the sounds they make.
- Respond to music in a variety of ways, e.g. through facial expression, movement, dance.
- Understand, and use, words related to dynamics and tempo, e.g. 'loud', 'quiet', 'fast', 'slow'.
- Make up their own words to describe sound, e.g. 'booming', 'tinkling'.
- Join in singing or chanting nursery rhymes, developing an awareness of alliteration, rhythm and rhyme.
- Build up a repertoire of, and have favourite, songs and rhymes.
- Repeat simple sound patterns using, for example, handclaps or drum beats.
- Make up their own rhythms.
- Move rhythmically.
- Make up their own songs and rhymes.
- Use instruments to accompany songs and rhymes.
- Interpret, or give meaning to, recorded or live music.
- Use words such as 'happy', 'sad', 'frightening' in relation to the atmosphere or mood of the music.
- Use their own made music or sounds to communicate ideas.
- Record their own music.
- Begin to use simple systems of notation, e.g. using coloured discs to represent sounds.

Display tips

- Posters and photographs of orchestras, bands, solo artists and instruments from different times and cultures.
- Evocative posters and pictures that encourage children to imagine or reproduce sounds, e.g. a thunderstorm, a firework display, horses galloping, cars racing on a track.
- Sheet music for familiar songs such as 'Twinkle, twinkle'.
- Interactive display including environmental sounds, photographs and tape recording. Children can match sounds to photographs.

Possible links with other areas of provision

Book area

Stories such as *Slinky Malinki* (Lynley Dodd) and *We're Going on a Bear Hunt* (Michael Rosen) help to develop children's awareness of rhythm. Clapping or beating a drum while chanting rhythmic, and sometimes rhyming, refrains to stories and poems can be a valuable learning experience.

Water area

Children will be able to produce a wealth of interesting sounds by pouring, splashing and dripping water, and may want to extend their investigations to other 'water sounds', such as rain, water gushing out of a tap, water disappearing down a plughole, waves, flowing water (in rivers and streams). Commercially produced recordings can help to introduce children to, or remind them of, sounds of the sea, torrential rainstorms and waterfalls. They will also enjoy making their own tapes of water sounds around the nursery.

Focus activities in the music and sound area

Counting sounds

Broaden children's experience of counting through their sense of hearing.

Counting sounds

Key areas of learning	Mathematical development (numbers for labels and for counting). Creative development (music).
Key early learning goals	Count reliably up to 10 everyday objects. Recognise and explore how sounds can be changed, sing simple songs from memory, recognise repeated sounds and sound patterns and match movements to music.
Resources needed/ enhancements to provision	Metal container. Wooden beads. Screen or piece of fabric.
Preparation	Make sure that children have plenty of concrete counting experiences and are familiar with the order of numbers one to ten. Plan lots of opportunities for matching one to one, e.g. place settings in the home corner, giving out pieces of fruit at snack time. Play games with children that will develop their listening skills, e.g. sounds lotto. Make sure that the area is free from noisy distractions when the activity takes place.
Key vocabulary	Number names one to ten. Loud, quiet.
Activity content	Listening attentively and counting as an adult, or another child, drops a number of beads into the metal container one at a time. Saying the number of beads that are in the container without looking. Checking the number by recounting the beads as they are taken out of the container.
Adult role	Stimulate children's interest in the activity by adding a 'magical' theme and presenting it as a 'show'. Introduce the beads and container at the beginning of the activity but then drop the beads into the container behind the screen or fabric. Demonstrate what is expected by counting the sounds of each bead dropping. When children know how many beads are in the container without even seeing them, they will think they are magicians themselves. Support children by counting with them when necessary. Alter the number of beads that are dropped into the container according to children's counting skills.
Follow-up ideas	Leave the resources in the music and sound area and encourage children to play the 'counting sounds' game with friends. Play games such as 'drum beats'. Children listen to, and count, the number of beats played on a drum and then take the same number of paces forward. This is repeated until they reach the other side of the room or outdoor area and run back to the starting point. Provide containers made from materials other than metal and encourage children to listen to the change in sound as they drop beads into the different containers. Provide a range of objects for children to drop into the metal container, e.g. rubber ball, cork, teaspoon. Encourage them to differentiate between sounds by guessing what has been dropped into the container.

Making shakers

Encourage children to experiment with sound and to make their own musical 'shakers'.

Making shakers

Key areas of learning	Knowledge and understanding of the world (exploration and investigation).
	Creative development (music, imagination).
Key early learning goals	Investigate objects and materials by using all of their senses as appropriate.
	Recognise and explore how sounds can be changed, sing simple songs from memory, recognise repeated sounds and sound patterns and match movements to music.
	Use their imagination in art and design, music, dance, imaginative play, role-play and stories.
Resources needed/ enhancements to provision	Empty, plastic film canisters with lids (photo-processing shops can often supply these in quantity; parents and carers can also be asked to collect them).
	A range of materials to put in the canisters, e.g. sand, gravel, small pebbles, pasta, rice, sunflower seeds, paper clips, beads, small shells. Sticky labels, pencils.
Preparation	Provide a range of maracas, rain makers etc. in the music area.
	Collect plenty of film canisters before starting the activity – some children will want to make lots of shakers.
	Find suitable storage containers for the materials. Plastic margarine tubs are ideal. Plastic spoons or small scoops are also a good idea.
Key vocabulary	Loud, quiet, rattle, shake.
	Encourage the use of descriptive and imaginative language, e.g. crackly, swishing, whooshing.
Activity content	Exploring the different materials.
	Selecting materials randomly to put in their canister.
	Choosing materials with the intention of creating a certain sound, e.g. rain.
	Mixing materials in the canister.
	Shaking the canisters, listening to and comparing sounds.
	Using shakers to accompany singing.
	Using shakers as props during story time to represent other sounds, e.g. snakes slithering, wind howling.
Adult role	Make your own shakers and talk about the sounds they produce.
	Ask questions such as 'What does your shaker sound like?' 'What kind of sound do think the sand will make?' 'Will it sound different if we add some pebbles?' 'Can you make a sound like a ticking clock?'
	Replenish stocks of materials when required.
	Encourage children to make a name label to identify their shaker.
Follow-up ideas	Encourage children to use their shakers together, e.g. sitting in a circle, one child begins to shake his or her canister and, in turn, other children join in to create a rainstorm starting with the patter of gentle rain and building up to a torrential downpour.
	Use the shakers to help develop children's awareness of rhythm, e.g. by tapping or shaking out their own names.
	Make an audiotape recording of the sounds produced by children's shakers.
	Offer a supply of empty canisters and encourage children to make shakers at home.

The outdoor area

Introduction to the area

Children need space to run, climb, balance and move freely. They need opportunities for strenuous and challenging activity on a daily basis. These experiences impact not only on children's future health but also on their intellectual development. Their bodies and brains develop together, and both need exercise. Children learn through being active and interacting with the world around them, through sensory and social experiences. The outdoor area can offer all these opportunities and, ideally, should be available to children as a choice for most of the session. Children who are able to be active when they need to will probably be calmer, and the introduction of a 'free flow' system between the indoor and outdoor areas is likely to lead to a reduction of behaviour issues in the setting as a whole.

Some settings do not have access to an outdoor area and, recognising the value of physical activity, teams go to great lengths to provide opportunities for gross motor development within the indoor area. Such plans do enhance children's opportunities but, however well resourced this area is, it will not offer children the range and quality of first-hand experiences they can have with access to a well-planned outdoor environment. Outside, physical learning is not the only learning that takes place – a well-planned area will offer rich opportunities across the whole curriculum. Links with all indoor areas of provision can provide extension opportunities and a chance for children to work on a larger scale with different materials, and resources do not have to be expensive. For example, construction projects in the outdoor area can involve large cardboard packaging boxes, recycled crates and tyres; decorators' brushes and buckets of water can be used to explore mark-making on surfaces such as walls and paving stones; sheets of wall lining paper attached to an outside wall can provide an ideal surface for a shared mural; and imaginative play and role-play in outdoor dens is always popular. Children are also, is most outdoor areas, free to make more noise than is acceptable inside. Experiments with voice sound and sounds made from everyday objects (see 'Equipment and materials') are important learning experiences and great fun.

The 'bad' weather is often given by practitioners as a reason for denying children access to the outdoor area. Given the nature of the British weather, this can mean that children's outdoor experiences are limited over quite a long period of time. The reluctance to go outside is usually on the part of the practitioner rather than the children, and if children are appropriately dressed, there is no reason why they should not be enjoying outdoor play in most conditions. In fact, our diverse weather conditions can provide a wealth of exciting learning opportunities for children (see 'Weather resources', 'Equipment and materials').

In most outdoor areas, it is possible to find a space that can be used as an exploration area where children are able to dig freely and make their own discoveries. An unused flowerbed, or a soil area 'reclaimed' from a grassed area, will provide hours of sensory experiences and fascinating investigations. Children will delight in finding worms as they dig, and the addition of a few logs will also attract creatures such as woodlice. Even the smallest of areas can be planned to include troughs and tyres containing materials such as compost, gravel and bark chippings. The 'free exploration' area may be linked to a 'planting and growing' area where children can sow seeds and care for plants. Some coniferous and deciduous trees and shrubs should also be planted if space allows. Hanging baskets attached to nearby walls offer another dimension, and a fixed shelf, or table, provides a surface for children to work at. Permanent areas such as these offer children the opportunity to carry out investigations over time and observe seasonal changes. The position of the areas should be thought about carefully. They should be sheltered from harsh winds and provide shade during sunny weather.

In order to be challenged, children do need to take some risks. The role of the practitioner in ensuring safety is in calculating the risks and weighing these up against the benefit of an activity. Some risks will be considered too high to contemplate, while others can be minimised with careful thought and perhaps some reorganisation. If children operate within an over-protective environment, they will not know their own capabilities and never learn to make their own judgements about safety. It is always a good idea, as a team, to complete a risk assessment for outdoor equipment and any activities that may pose a risk. Through the process of risk assessment, staff awareness of potential hazards will be raised, definitions of

The digging area

what is an 'acceptable risk' agreed and ways of reducing unacceptable risks discussed.

The outdoor area should be viewed not merely as another area of provision but as a vital part of the whole nursery setting, offering a range of provision and opportunities for learning across the curriculum. For this reason no 'Possible links with other areas of provision' section is included in this chapter. Planning will include organising areas within the outdoor space. The following areas are suggested:

- A quiet area where children can read, chat, observe or reflect.
- An area where children can run freely or ride wheeled toys.
- A free digging area, cultivated garden area and 'wild area'.
- An area designated for climbing and balancing equipment and activity (a safe 'landing' surface is needed in this area).
- A large construction area (e.g. crates, tyres).
- There must be enough space in the remaining area to include other provision (reflecting and extending indoor areas) such as paint, small construction, imaginative play, mark-making equipment, sand and water. When planning the space, it is important to remember that children will probably be working on a larger scale than in the indoor areas – water investigations particularly can take up an extensive area with the addition of extra trays and pipes.

Basic resources

Furniture and storage

- A large, lockable wooden shed or metal store positioned in a convenient place in the outdoor area is the ideal for outdoor equipment. It is worth fitting shelves, hooks and brackets in the store to maximise the space. If equipment has to be kept inside, it should be as near as possible to the door. The easier it is to access and put out equipment, the more likely it is that the outdoor area is used to its full potential.
- Plastic storage boxes, labelled. Large, wheeled boxes.
- Appropriate trolley for equipment such as hoops and balls.
- 'Wardrobe' trolley for dressing-up clothes.
- Table, chairs.

Equipment and materials

Much of the equipment that will be present in a well-resourced outdoor area has already been listed in previous 'area of provision' chapters. Only resources that are specific to the outdoor area are included in the list below.

- Natural features, such as willow tunnels, rustic seating, logs, large stones.
- A range of plants, shrubs and trees. (Practitioners should check that all plants, shrubs and trees are safe for children to touch before including them.) Sensory experiences are important – herbs and fragrant flowers will appeal to children's sense of smell.
- Gravel, bark chippings, sand, compost, 'grow bags'.
- Plant pots, troughs, seed trays, watering cans, garden sieves, hanging baskets.
- Trowels, spades, scoops, rakes, hoes.
- Spare wellington boots.
- Climbing and balancing equipment, e.g. frames, slides, ladders, planks and large blocks.
- Small equipment, such as beanbags, balls (varying sizes, weights and textures), bats, racquets, skipping ropes, hoops, quoits, stilts.
- Fabric tunnels, plastic 'barrels'.
- Recycled resources, such as crates, traffic cones, tyres.
- Wheeled toys, such as tricycles (including two-seaters), scooters, trucks. Number plates attached to the front of these toys can then be matched to corresponding numbered 'parking bays'.
- Road signs, zebra crossing, traffic lights.
- Dressing-up clothes, such as police and traffic warden uniforms, builders' hats.
- Sand tray or permanent sandpit.
- Shallow builders' tray.
- Water trays, buckets and troughs.
- Half pipes, pipes, plastic guttering (readily available at little expense from DIY stores).
- Portable mark-making box (see Chapter 5).
- Large chalkboard, chalks.
- Decorators' brushes, water containers.
- Walkie-talkies.
- Lengths of fabric, den 'frame'.
- Book boxes containing a range of books, including information books about wildlife, weather etc.
- Magnifying glasses, 'bug' boxes, binoculars, telescopes.
- Soft mats, rugs, carpet offcuts or sample squares.

- A range of everyday objects that can be used to explore sound, such as pans, pan lids, plastic bottles, tin trays and plates. Objects can be hung on fences, branches or purpose-built frames, and wooden or metal spoons used as beaters.

Weather resources

It is a good idea to prepare 'weather boxes', which can be brought out spontaneously to support children's interest in weather conditions. Appropriate pictures, posters, fiction and non-fiction books could also be included.

Rain

- Umbrellas, splash suits, rain hats, wellington boots.
- Cooking foil (an umbrella covered with foil will produce loud and exciting rain sounds), tin trays.
- Rainmakers (can be purchased in natural or man-made materials).
- Funnels, containers, measuring cylinders, tubes, half pipes (for building rain collection systems).
- Absorbent paper (for 'catching' raindrops).
- Waterproof and non-waterproof materials.
- Audiotape or CD of rainstorm sounds.

Sun

- Sunhats, sun umbrellas.
- Tents, beach shelters.
- Shadow puppets.
- Sundials.
- Chalk (for drawing around children's own shadows).
- Hats and pieces of fabric that children can use to change the shape or character of their shadow.

Frost/ice

- Ice cubes (varying shapes and sizes containing, for example, sequins, buttons, pieces of vegetable) – these can be prepared in advance and kept in the freezer.
- Ice lolly sticks, lolly moulds, juice. Making ice lollies will reinforce children's learning about the effects of freezing water.
- Objects that can be left outside overnight in freezing conditions – children can observe the changes that take place in different materials as they are frozen.
- Absorbent paper – this can be used to take prints from frost patterns on windows.

Wind

- Windsocks, windmills, kites.
- Crêpe paper ribbons (for children to 'fly').
- Fabric ribbons to tie to tree branches in windy weather.
- Wind chimes.
- Everyday objects (e.g. metal spoons, whisks, old necklaces), coat-hangers and thread for making 'sound' mobiles.
- Tubes for children to blow through and make 'wind' noises.
- Audiotapes or CDs of wind sounds.

Snow

- Spades, scoops, snow shovels, trowels.
- Toy vehicles, such as diggers and ploughs.
- Plastic containers, buckets and moulds (small, rectangular margarine tubs make effective 'snow brick' moulds).
- Plastic 'squeezy' bottles – filled with warm water, these can be used to make patterns in the snow.
- Flour 'sifters' containing powder paint. Children can 'shake' patterns into the snow and watch the effects as the paint 'spreads'.
- Shoes and boots with interesting tread patterns are useful for making different footprints in the snow.
- Black card or paper (for 'catching' snowflakes).
- Magnifying glasses for examining snowflakes.
- Arctic small world equipment.

What will children do and learn?

Listed below are just a few of the learning experiences available to children in the outdoor area.

- Move freely.
- Explore space and equipment confidently.
- Show awareness of others.
- Develop gross motor skills and coordination.
- Respond to sensory experiences.
- Show interest in seasonal changes and changes in the weather.
- Explore materials and the natural world around them.
- Engage in scientific investigations (e.g. using water to move balls from one place to another).
- Talk about observations.
- Be familiar with some of the conditions necessary to plant and animal growth and well-being.
- Ask questions and use books to find out information.
- Engage in, and initiate, imaginative play and role-play.
- Join in games such as 'hopscotch' and 'What's the time, Mr Wolf?'
- Explore mark-making in a range of contexts and on a large scale.

Display tips

- It is possible to display pictures and posters (preferably laminated) in the outdoor area, and a surface as simple as a brick wall can provide the backdrop. Hooks attached to the wall, or a line with pegs, can be used to hold pictures.
- Photographs hung from tree branches also provide an interesting focus.
- Covering windows with pictures should be avoided, as this will obstruct children's view of the outside world as they play inside.
- Free-standing shelves, or shelves attached to walls, can provide a useful surface for displaying children's 'finds' or constructions.
- If there are ample boards in the indoor area, it is a good idea to designate one for displaying photographs of outdoor activities.

Focus activities in the outdoor area

Buried treasure

Children love searching for treasure, and this activity will inspire imaginative ideas, as well as introducing them to simple map reading.

Buried treasure

Key areas of learning	Knowledge and understanding of the world (sense of place). Creative development (responding to experiences, and expressing and communicating ideas).
Key early learning goals	Observe, find out about and identify features in the place they live and the natural world. Express and communicate their ideas, thoughts and feelings by using a widening range of materials, suitable tools, imaginative play, role-play, movement, designing and making, and a variety of songs and musical instruments.
Resources needed/ enhancements to provision	A simple map or plan of the outdoor area with the buried treasure marked. An anonymous letter (with treasure map enclosed) addressed to children explaining that some treasure has been hidden in their garden. A 'treasure box' (a plastic, wooden or metal box with a lid). 'Treasure', e.g. jewellery, coins, keys, ornaments. (Check that all objects are safe for children to handle and play with.) Spades, scoops, rakes.
Preparation	Select a position in the outdoor area where the 'treasure box' can be buried, perhaps the designated digging area, or a tyre filled with compost. Make sure that there is no visible sign of the buried treasure. Make copies of the map so that children can have their own.
Key vocabulary	Near, next to, behind, in front of, in, on, under.
Activity content	Looking at, and discussing, the map. Matching pictures or symbols on the map to features in the outdoor area (e.g. gate, path, tree, flower bed, climbing frame). Identifying the location of the buried treasure. Digging up the treasure box. Exploring the treasure. Sharing ideas about who the treasure belongs to, why it has been buried etc. Giving imaginative meaning to treasure items. Engaging in imaginative play and story making.
Adult role	Stimulate interest in the activity by reading the anonymous letter and looking at the map with children. Ask questions such as 'Who do you think has sent the letter?' 'Why have they sent it to us?' 'What do you think we should do?' Discuss features on the map with children and help them to locate these in the outdoor area. Support children's play as it progresses by providing further resources (e.g. a large cardboard box to make a ship to escape with the treasure, or clipboards and paper to draw new maps as the treasure is hidden in a different place). Scribe children's ideas and take photographs of their play.
Follow-up ideas	Use children's ideas, and photographs taken during the activity, to make a storybook. Share the book with children and keep it in the book corner. Write letters with children to the owner of the treasure. Encourage parents and carers to talk with their children about features of the local environment and perhaps to make a simple map showing their route to nursery.

Making tracks!

Take advantage of the space in the outdoor area to explore pattern and line on the bikes.

Making tracks!

Key areas of learning	Physical development (movement, sense of space).
	Creative development (exploring media and materials).
Key early learning goals	Move with control and coordination.
	Show awareness of space, themselves and others.
	Explore colour, texture, shape, form and space in two or three dimensions.
Resources needed/ enhancements to provision	Large roll of paper (thick wall lining paper is ideal).
	Large quantity of mixed paint.
	Wheeled toys, such as bikes, scooters, pedal cars.
Preparation	Secure a length of paper to the ground in the outdoor area. Make sure this is positioned away from other activities. There may be enough space to provide two parallel paper 'roads'.
	Mix plenty of paint, but make sure that supplies are stored in a place where they won't be knocked over.
Key vocabulary	Straight, curved, wavy, zigzag, line, turn, steer, space.
Activity content	Riding wheeled toys through paint and showing interest in the effect created on the paper.
	Experimenting with effects, e.g. steering the bike to the left and right to create a wavy line.
	Comparing tyre patterns.
	Observing as others add to the pattern.
Adult role	Explain the importance of all riding in the same direction, and of waiting until the person in front has finished their turn.
	Renew paper, and provide more paint, as necessary.
	Talk with children about the different patterns and lines their tyres have made.
	If children's shoes become covered in paint, wipe them before they go inside.
Follow-up ideas	Use wellington boots with different tread designs to make patterns on paper. Encourage children to wear the wellington boots, stand in paint and then walk, hop, run or skip along the paper.
	Encourage children to look at the patterns they make on tarmac or paving stones as they ride bikes through rain puddles.
	Look at the tracks made by toy vehicles in wet sand or dough.

© Community Playthings Ph: 0800387457.
  Used by permission

Also available...

 David Fulton Publishers

Planning Children's Play and Learning in the Foundation Stage

Jane Drake

> 'This exciting new book is written by a practising nursery teacher using her wealth of experience. It will be welcomed by all those who are either studying or working with children within the foundation stage. There is appropriate emphasis on the importance of play and the planning and organisation of a stimulating environment, both indoors and outdoors. Case studies bring to life examples of good organisational practice, and planning of focused activities is considered in detail.
>
> There are clear links to the relevant early learning goals throughout. The practical sections on display and home links, along with straightforward, logical approach to the planning and assessment cycle are an added bonus.'
> **Nursery Education**

Contents: Introduction; Planning the learning environment and quality areas of provision; Planning focus activities; Starting points for developing learning through focus activities; Establishing and developing positive links with home; Planning display as part of the curriculum; Observing children's play, assessing learning and keeping useful records; Looking forward.

£16.00 • Paperback • 160 pages • 1-85346-752-9 • 2001

Literacy Play for the Early Years

Collette Drifte

This series of books helps young children in the Early Years develop their literacy skills by bringing together the early learning goals of the foundation stage and the national literacy strategy objectives, using structured play, games and fun activities to put across the relevant teaching points in an enjoyable way, while simultaneously nurturing a love of literature. Each book presents:

- structured activities that use the texts as a basis to focus on specific literacy goals and objectives
- planning and preparation for each literacy session, including materials needed and scripted sessions
- ideas for working and playing with the whole group and smaller groups to consolidate the literacy skill
- extension ideas and activities to bring in wider aspects of the Early Learning Goals and the NLS objectives

Book 1: Learning through Fiction

£12.00 • Paperback • 96 A4 pages • 1-85346-956-4 • 2003

Book 2: Learning Through Non-Fiction

£12.00 • Paperback • 96 A4 pages • 1-85346-957-2 • 2003

Book 3: Learning Through Poetry

£12.00 • Paperback • 112 A4 pages • 1-85346-958-0 • 2003

Book 4: Learning Through Phonics

£14.00 • Paperback • 104 A4 pages + CD
1-85346-959-9 • 2003

 with CD

Meeting the Early Learning Goals Through Role Play
A Practical Guide for Teachers and Assistants

Marie Aldridge

This book offers step-by-step guidance to help busy practitioners create meaningful role play that will delight young children, enhance learning, *and* link to the Early Learning Goals.

It shows exactly how to plan, organise and implement the role play activities and gives suggestions on setting the scene, resources required and introducing each new topic. The activities have been tried, tested and thoroughly enjoyed in the busy nursery where the author works.

Busy teachers and assistants can simply dip into the appropriate section and get on with the fun.

c. £18.00 • Paperback • 200 A4 pages
1-84312-036-4 • June 2003

Planning the Pre-5 Setting
Practical Ideas and Activities for the Nursery

Christine Macintyre and **Kim McVitty**

This is a practical guide to organising, resourcing and teaching in pre-school settings. The book draws on the excitement created by the natural calendar and the children's own interests to provide learning opportunities suited to the individual's needs.

Contents: Introduction; Settling in; Planning the first meeting with parents and children; Year Plan, Section 2; Planning Learning - yearly, monthly, weekly and daily plans, Section 3; setting up and resourcing the basic areas; Adapting the resources, Section 4; Daily planning meetings, Section 5; How to record a child's progress; How to identify and support children with SEN, Section 6; Parents as partners.

c. £16.00 • Paperback • 124 A4 pages
1-84312-058-5 • June 2003

Outdoor Play in the Early Years
Management and Innovation
SECOND EDITION

Helen Bilton

> 'Helen Bilton's much needed and excellent book has filled a gap in the literature about outdoor play. I would recommend it as essential reading for all who work with children in the early years or make decisions about the appropriateness of settings.'
> **Early Education**

This book stimulates and challenges practitioners to develop a truly effective teaching and learning environment by providing detailed guidance and discussions on organising, managing and resourcing their outdoor area.

This new edition now includes a resource and equipment list, examples of assessment, running records, planning and a suggested outdoor area layout.

Contents: Introduction; An environment for teaching and learning; A combined environment; The outdoor environment - an historical perspective; Design and layout; Learning bays; Children using the outdoor environment; The role of the adult; Modes of learning.

£15.00 • Paperback • 144 pages • 1-85346-952-1 • 2002

David Fulton Publishers, The Chiswick Centre, 414 Chiswick High Road, London W4 5TF
Tel: 020 8996 3610   Fax: 020 8996 3622   E-mail: orders@fultonpublishers.co.uk
www.fultonpublishers.co.uk